Drawing
Landscape

By

Prosenjit & Arundhati

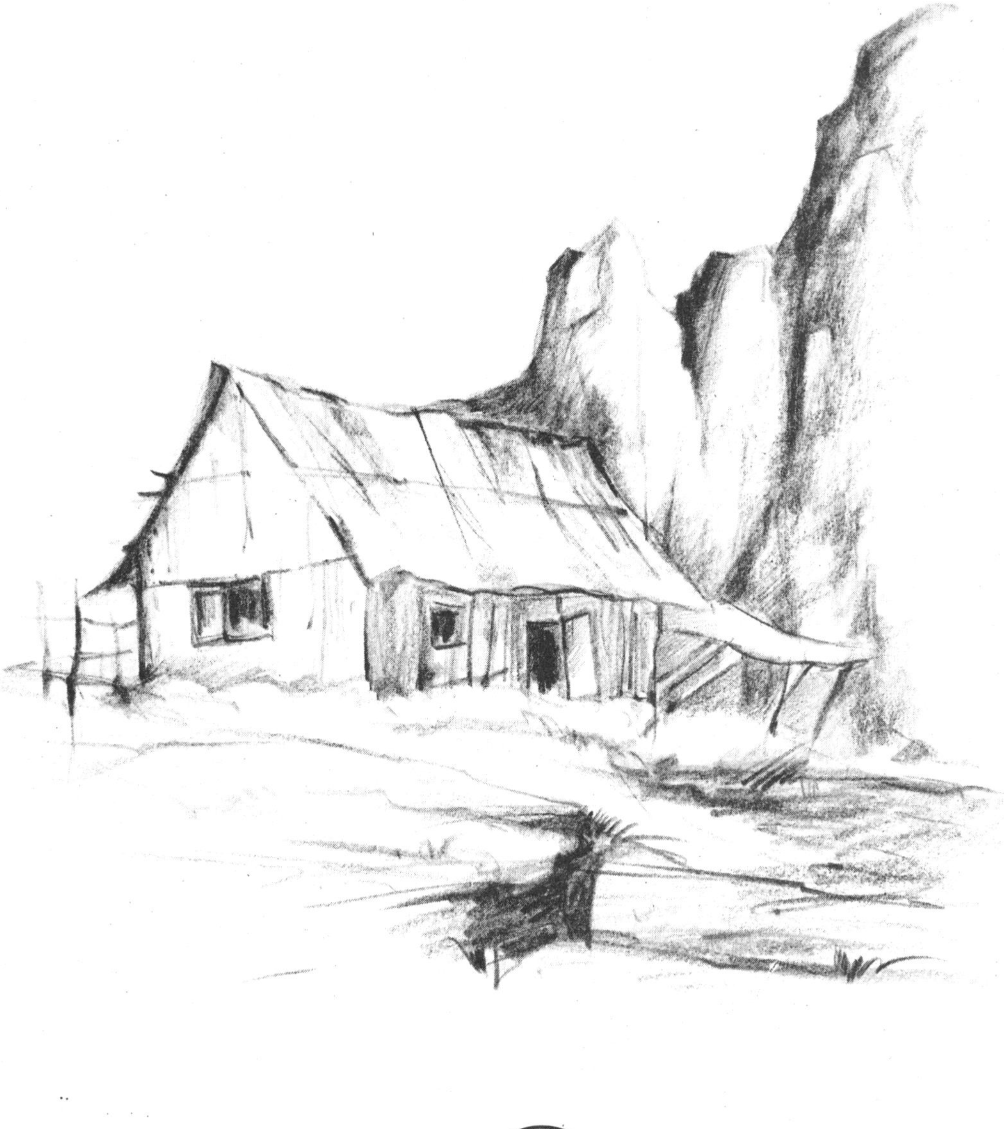

UNICORN BOOKS

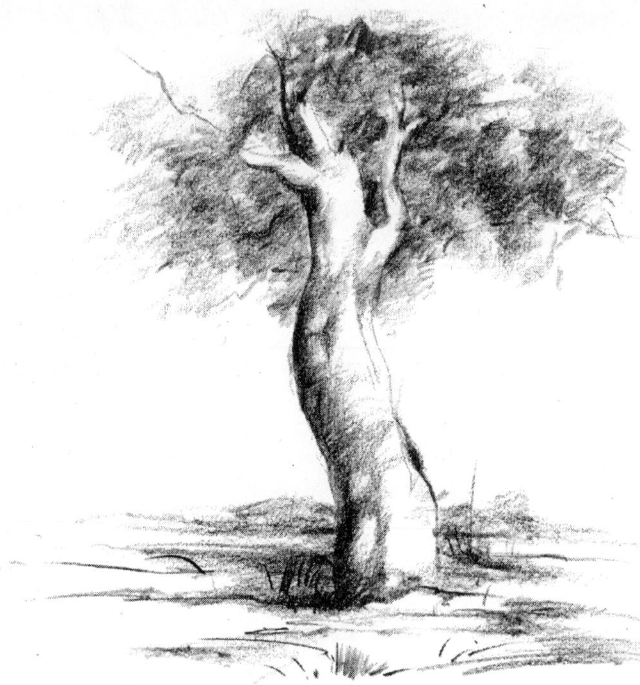

ISBN: 978-81-7806-154-2
Drawing Landscape
UNICORN BOOKS (P) Ltd., F-2/16, Ansari Road,
Darya Ganj, New Delhi-110002
Phones: 23262683, 23250704, Fax: 23257790
Email: unicornbooks@vsnl.com
Website: www.unicornbooks.in • www.kidscorner.in

Contents

Introduction

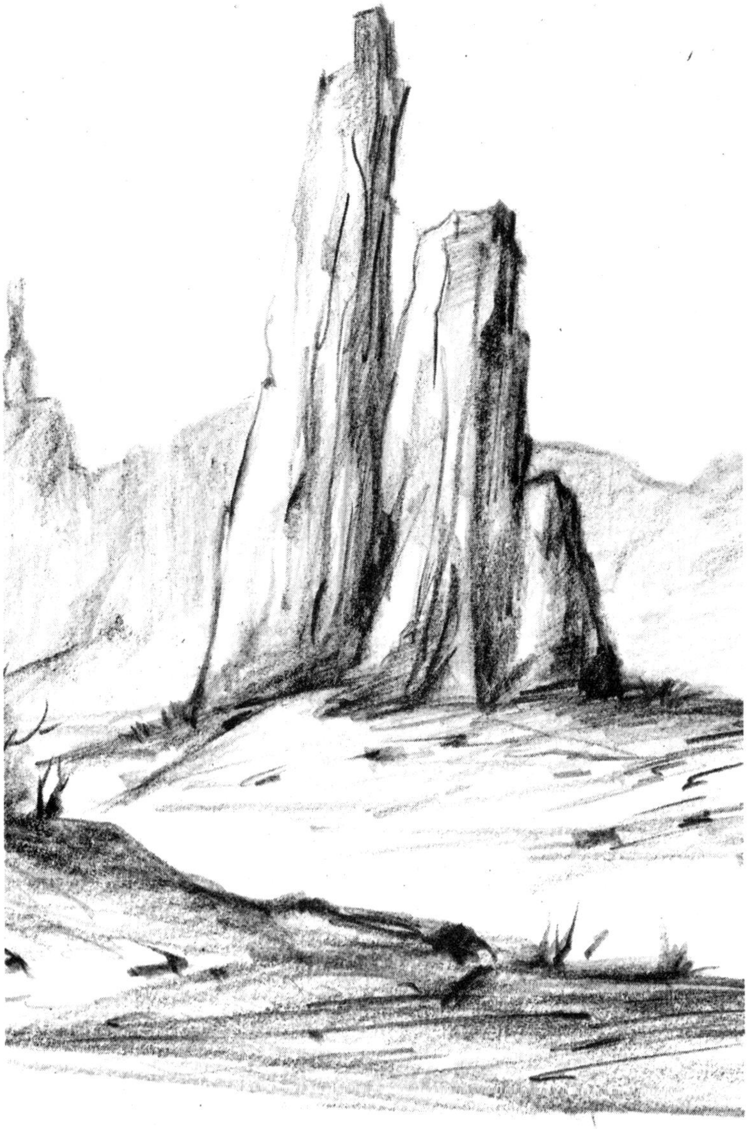

Nature provides almost everything to us. Landscape study involves all these elements that we find in nature.

Studying Landscape involves volume, line drawing, tone drawing, pencil shading and colour. While studying Landscape we shall combine the light source and the perspective of the subject. It also makes us understand the character of the subjects like Tree, Water, Mountain etc. We also study the hidden character of the particular elements.

While drawing a Landscape, do keep all these above mentioned points in your mind and go through this book as it will make you able to grasp the basics of Landscape drawing and other related aspects properly.

We assure you that you will be able to grasp and see a big change in your artistic talents by the time you reach the last page.

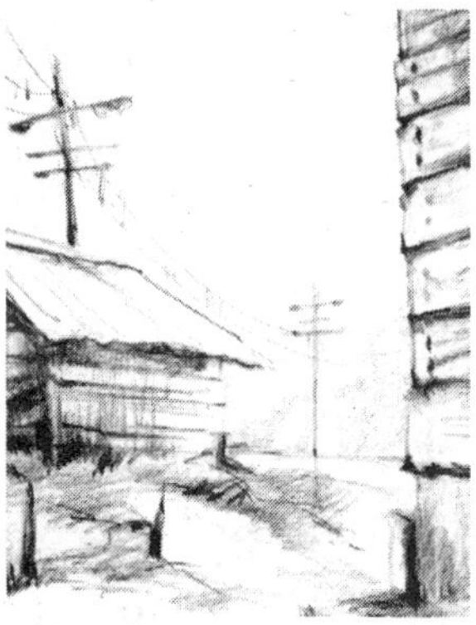

Draw in an easy manner. With the passage of time you will become perfect in handing your pencil and in using your paper and its texture. White cartridge paper, tinted paper and mount board are some of the working surface I have used in these drawings. Pencils which will give you great results and satisfaction are 2B,4B,6B and black conte crayon. Which one "you" would like to use to draw a certain thing is up to you.

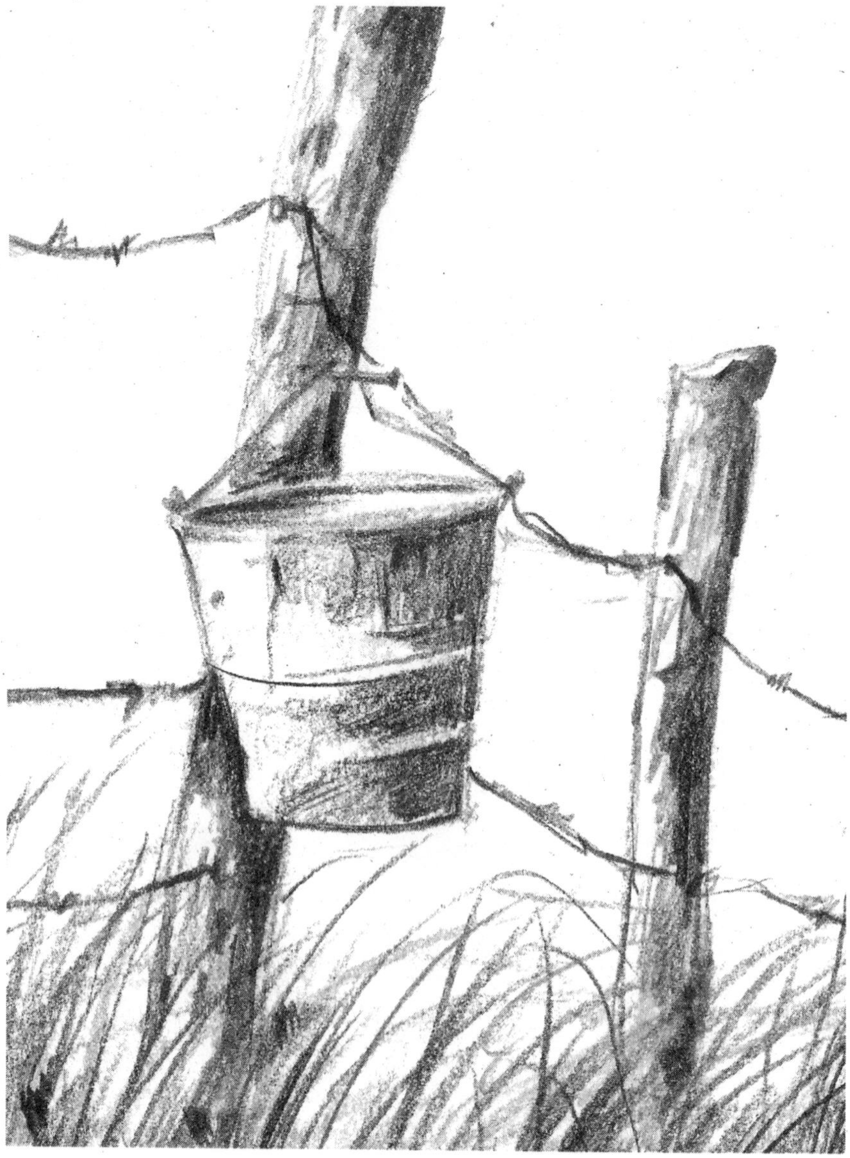

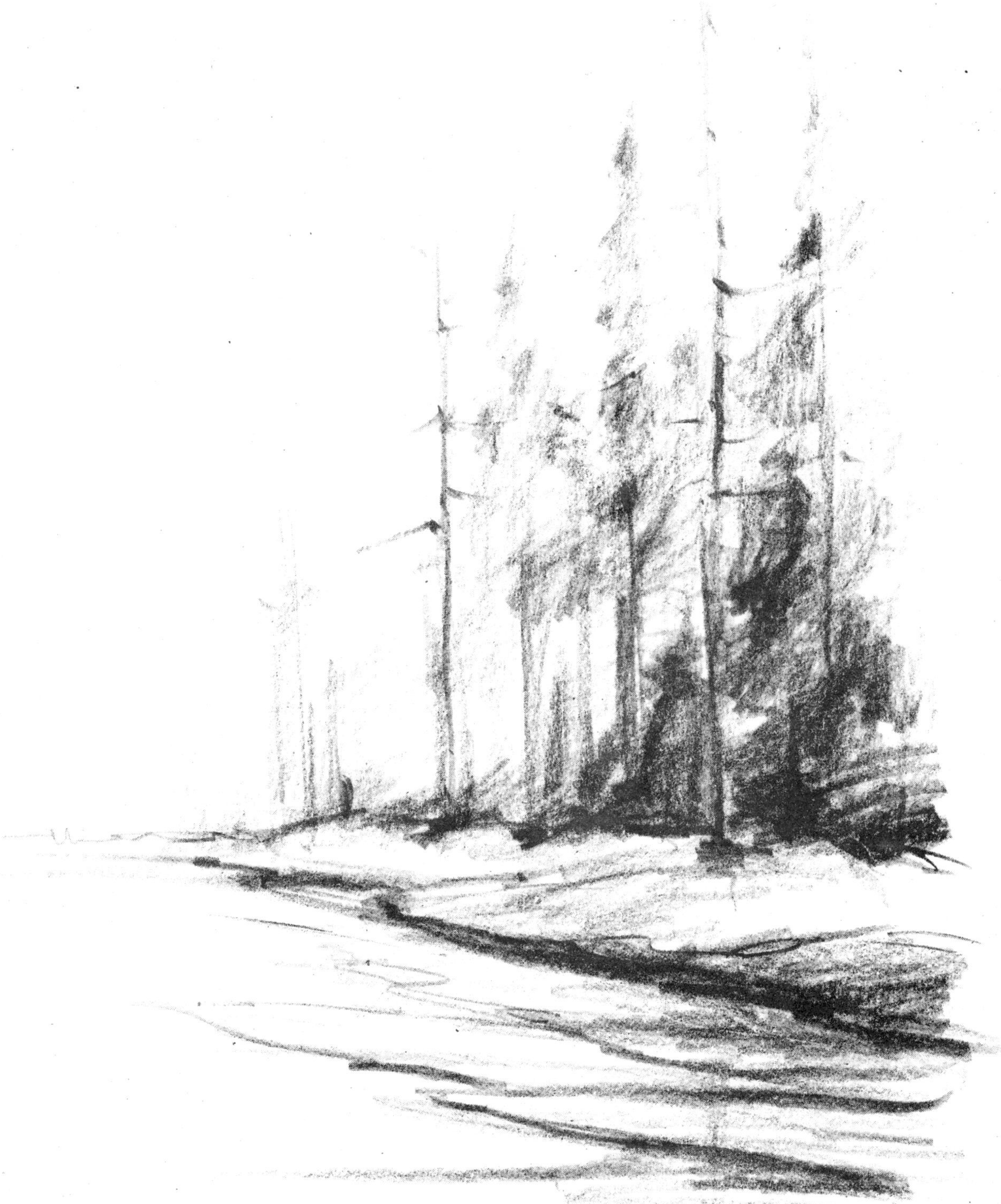

Basic Things of Drawing

The small drawing at the lower right shows the exact procedure that was followed in the main drawing. The lines from the light source through A, and from the vanishing point of shadows through B, meet at the point of C. Thus C is the point of the cast shadow. Always think of a triangle while composing of light source, angle of the light source and the vanishing point.

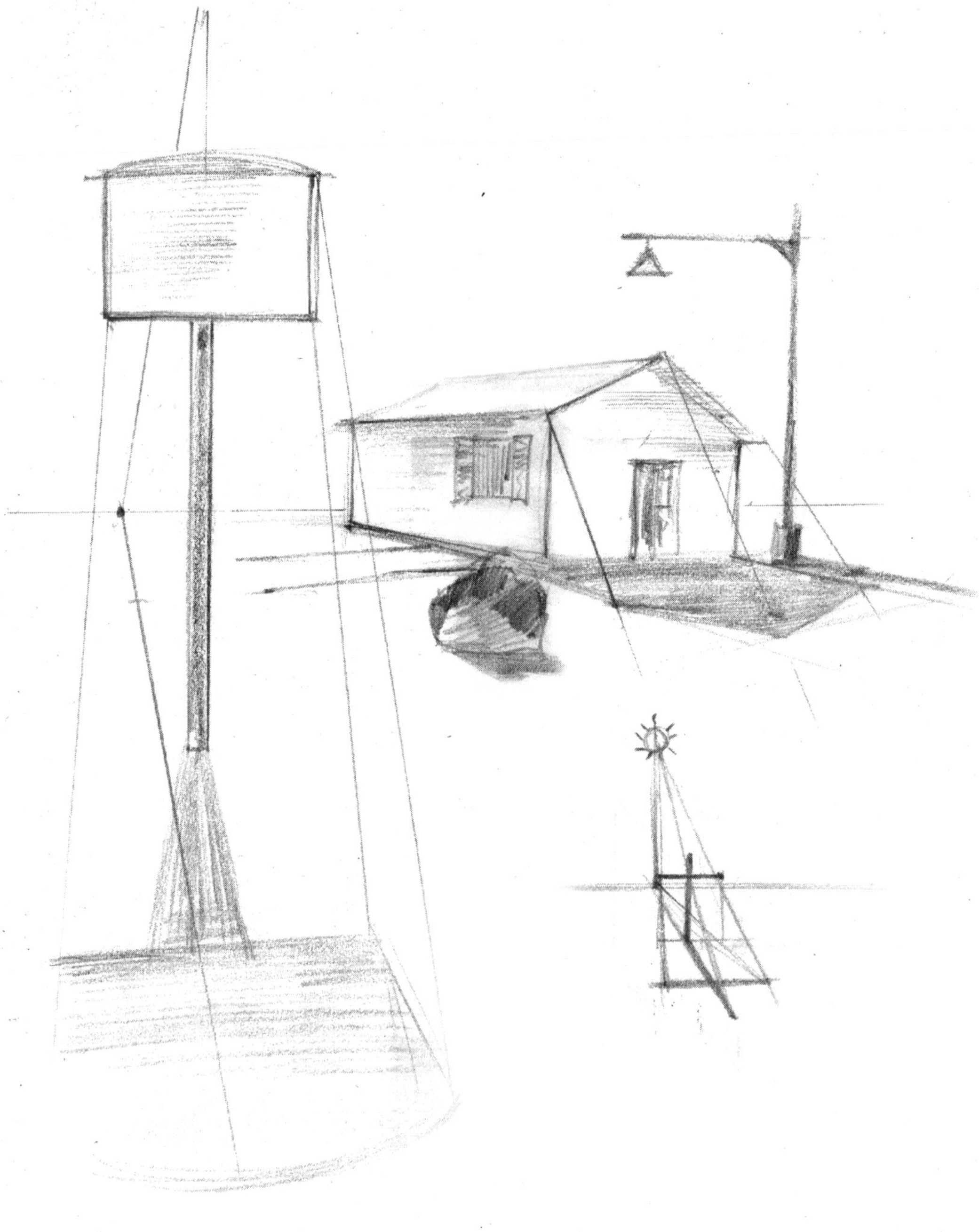

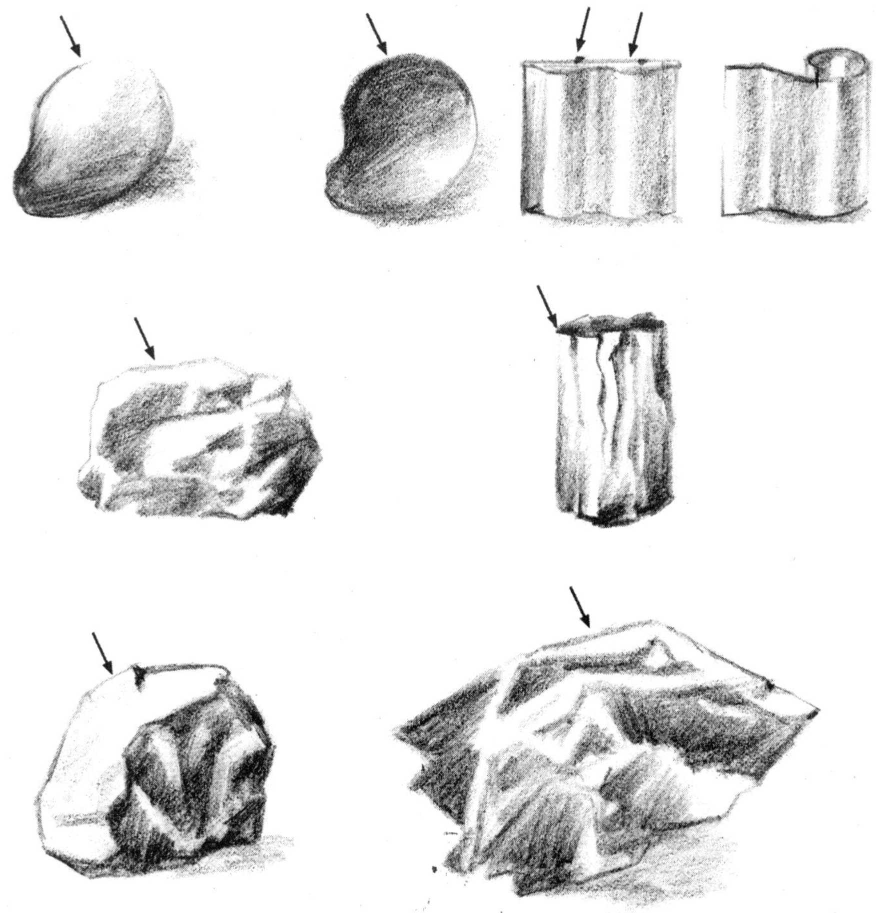

A drawing like the one shown above cannot be drawn or painted convincingly without a study of the light on its planes. The camera can give only the superficial effects. We should always search for the broader planes upon which these confusing details lie. Since the light changes so rapidly, it is practical to make a quick sketch drawing like the one at the top of the page, to record the main planes of the light, halftone, and shadow. This gives a basis for building the solid effects later. Careful study of this page will reveal the fact that any type of surface form can be rendered by duplicating the effect of light and shadow as they occur. Every material or surface has its own characteristic effect. Every effect is made up of light, halftone and shadow. If we study the subject and can define those elements clearly and can then fit them properly, we have a re-created form and also the effects of the material of which it is composed. In the drawings above, arrows indicate the direction of the light. Set up a number of subjects composed of a variety of materials and render the effects.

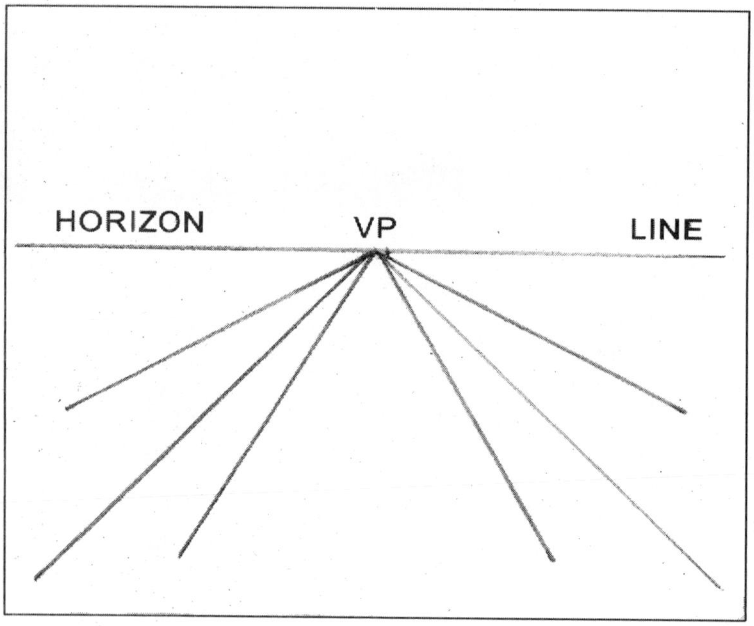

In this graph is shown a one point perspective, which is used when you are looking straight out to the sea. If you are sure of your perspective, it is a good idea to draw a few simple lines on your canvas and then build your composition on the perspective lines. As you become more familiar with the perspective, you can imagine the lines are there, and can feel the perspective as you draw.

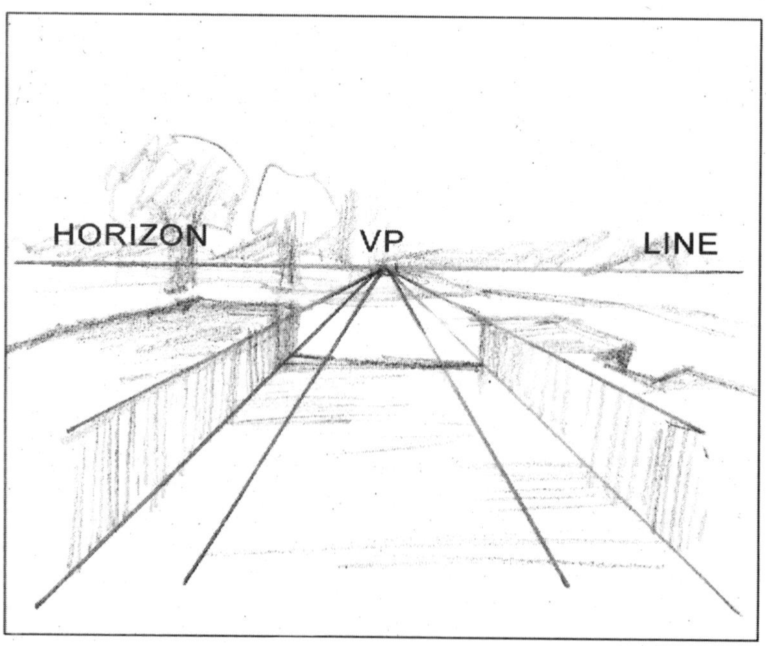

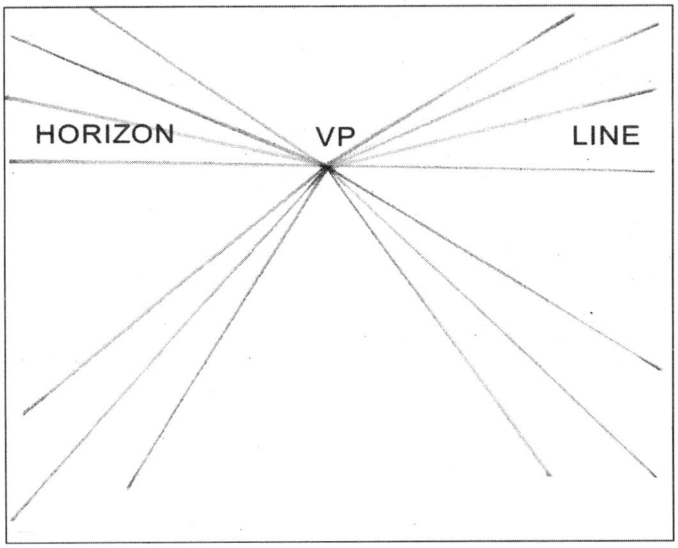

This graph shows how to draw your subject on top of the perspective lines.Perspective is very important in all types of realistic painting. To get depth, note that every thing gets smaller in the distance, even the clouds. Also take notice that the waves and clouds are parallel to the horizon line. Every thing else converges to the vanishing point.

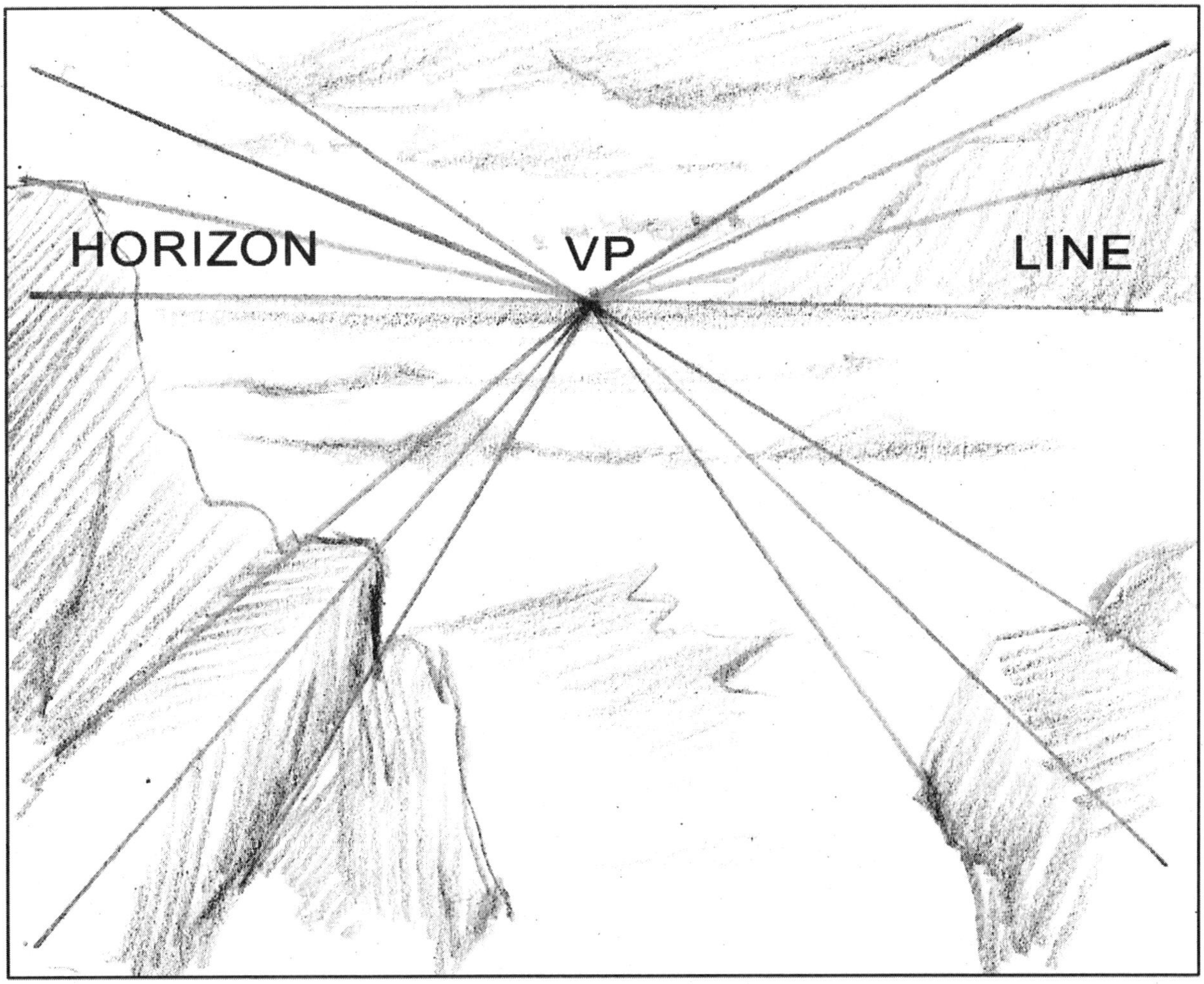

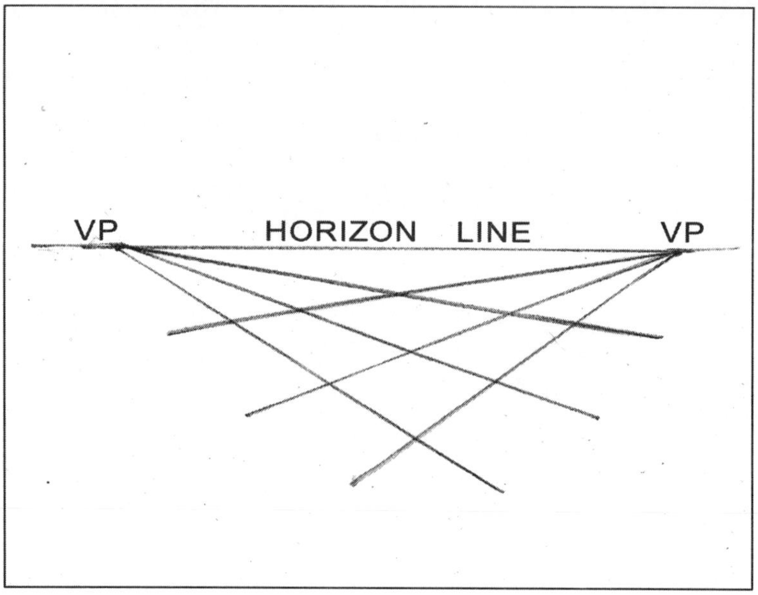

This graph shows two point perspectives, which means, two vanishing points. Two point perspective is used when you look to the right or left of your subject. You can have both vanishing points in your picture, or one in and the other out, or both out. They do not have to be at equal distances from the center. Cut a 3 inc square out of a piece of paper, and move it around on the drawing below. This will make it easier to understand.

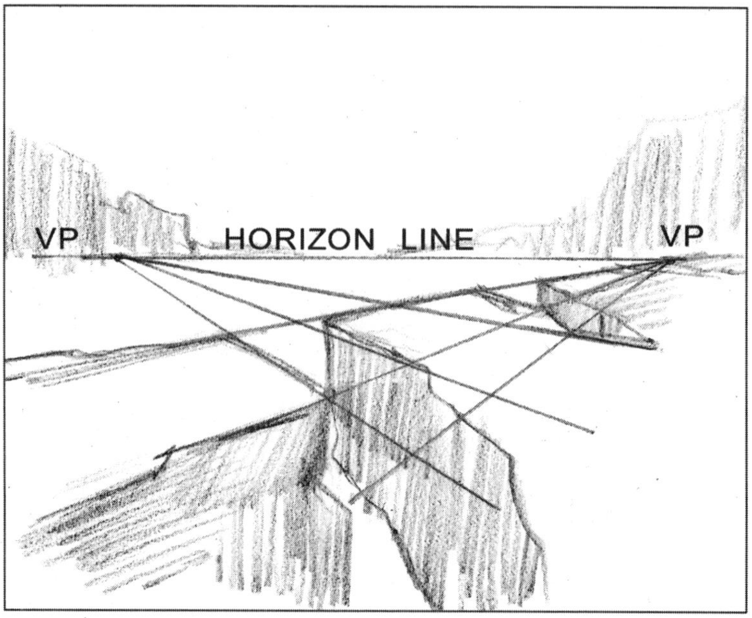

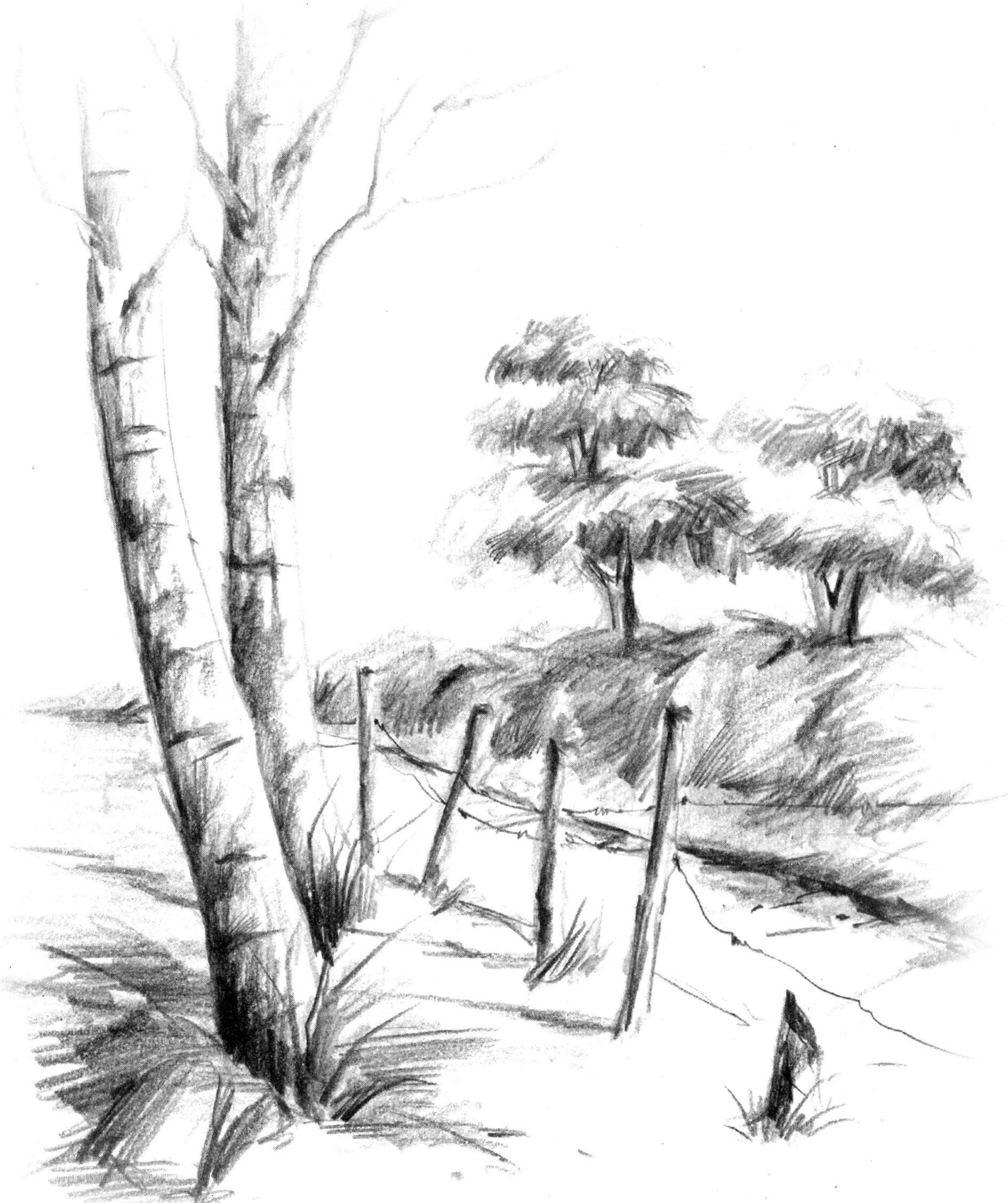

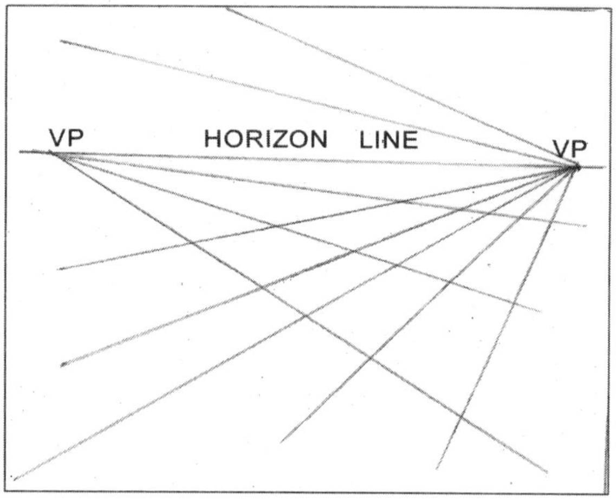

In this graph, the clouds, waves, rock and the water on the beach are going to the right vanishing point. The other rock and main land are going to the left vanishing point. The further away every thing is, the more parallel to the horizon line it gets. The water coming up on the beach can be a free form line, but still roughly following the perspective line. The same goes for the shapes of rocks.

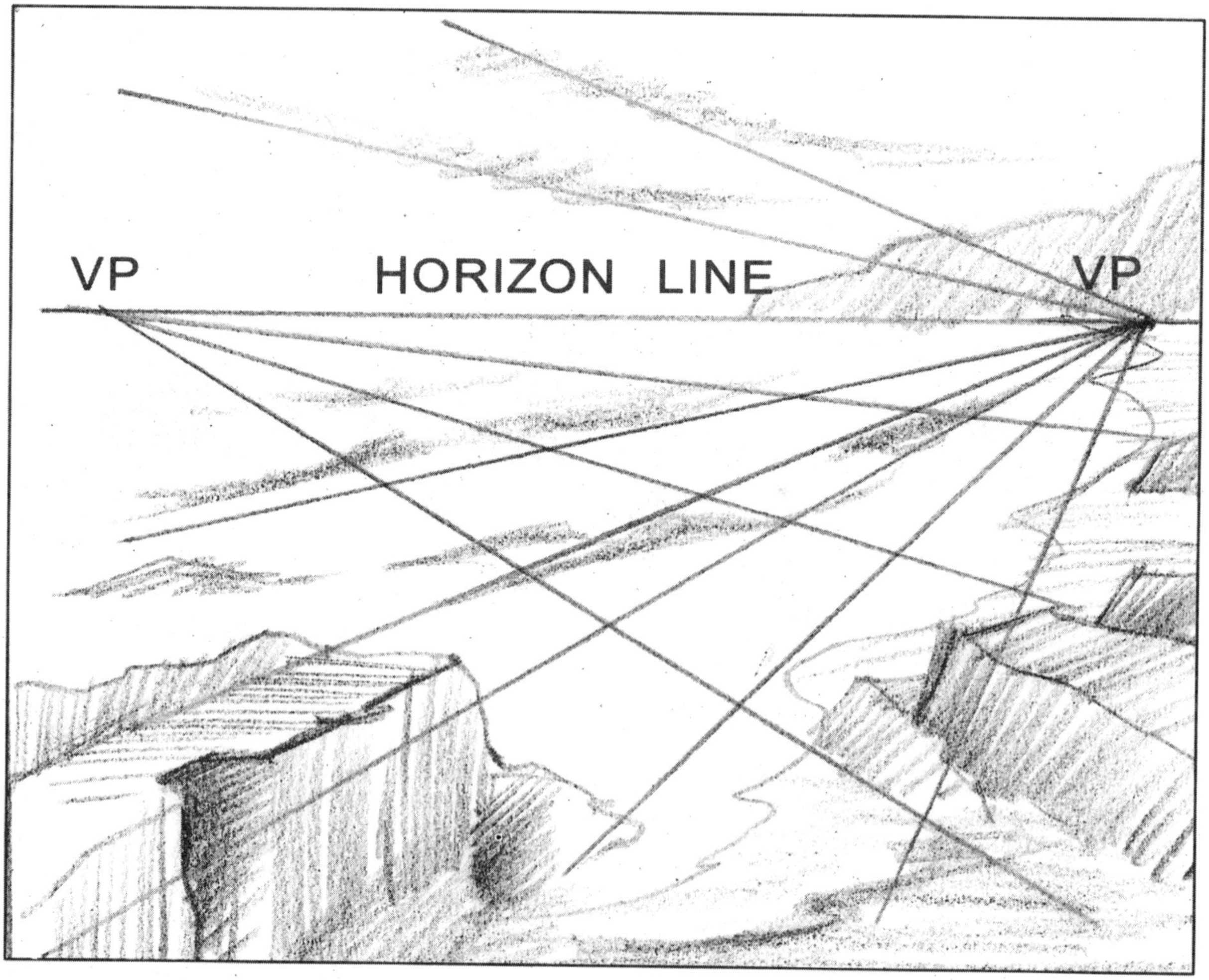

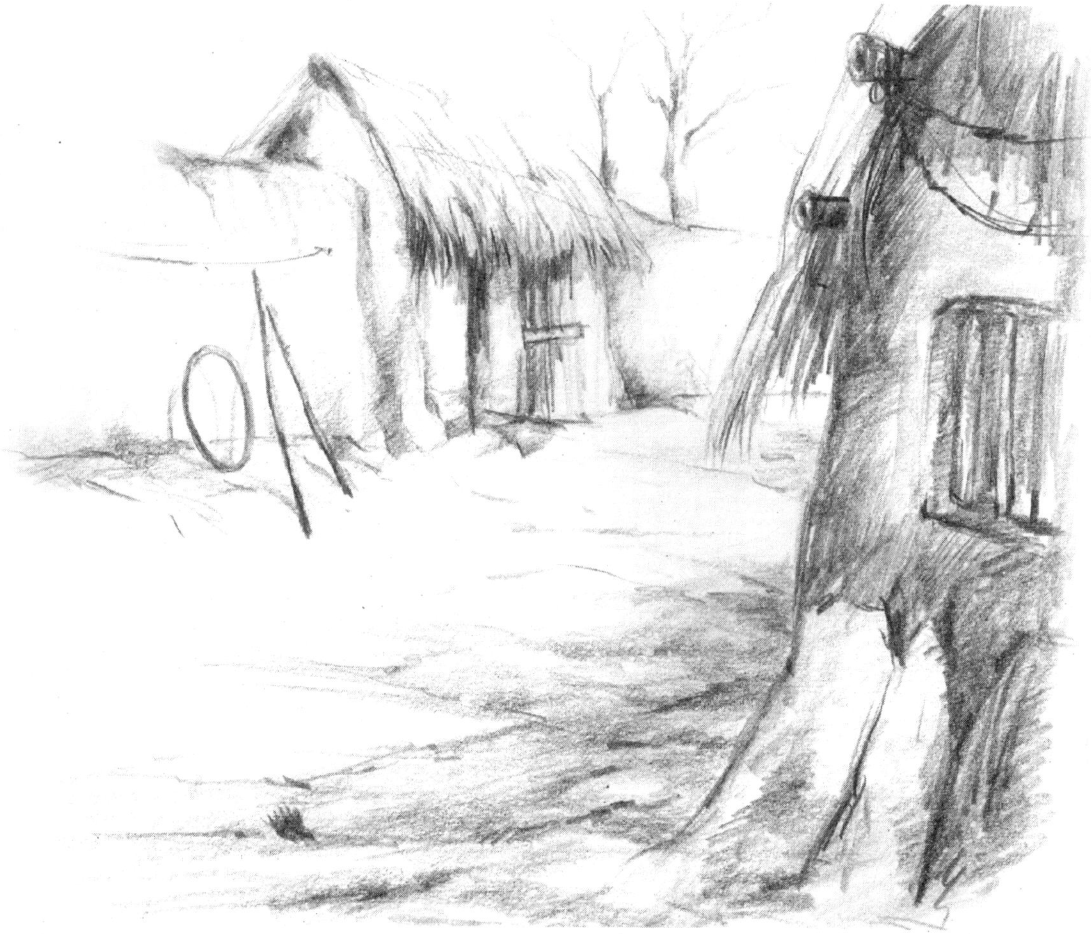

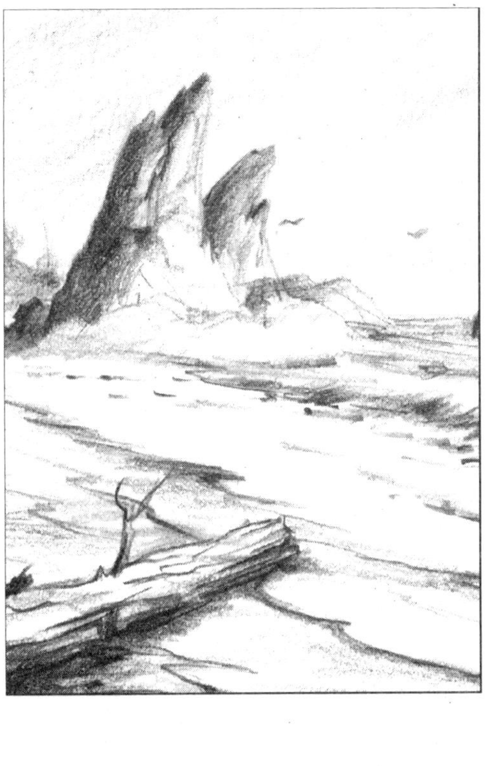

What a drawing can express without speaking, we need hundred words to say that very same thing, So, what I would like to say to you, it will be though sketches. This book is not about difficulties in drawing or to turn you into an expert of Nature Drawing. Take a long hard look at the subject and check the proportion and negative space then simply start drawing it on the paper.

In this diagram you can make a proper landscape using the following steps.....

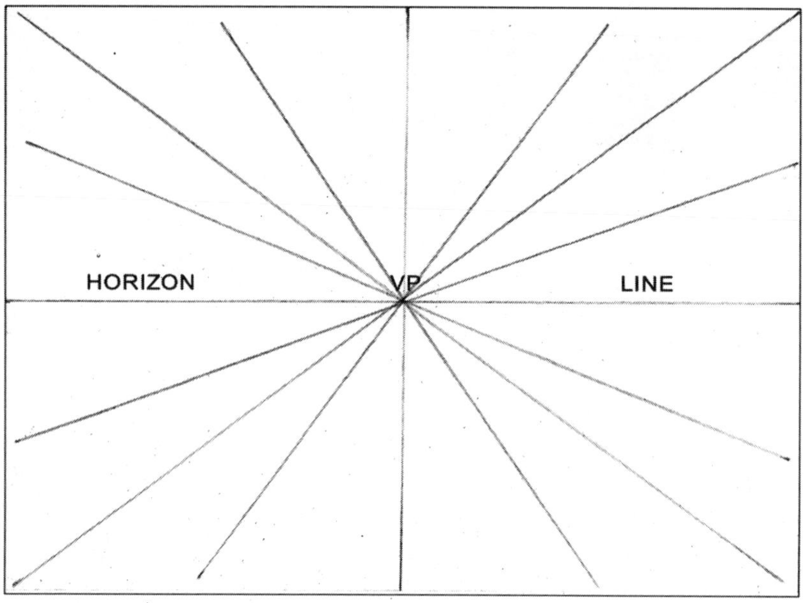

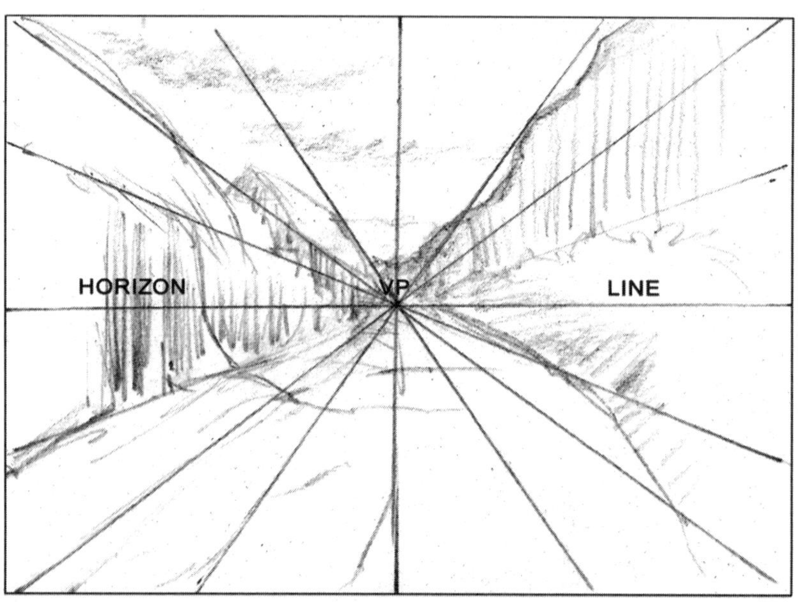

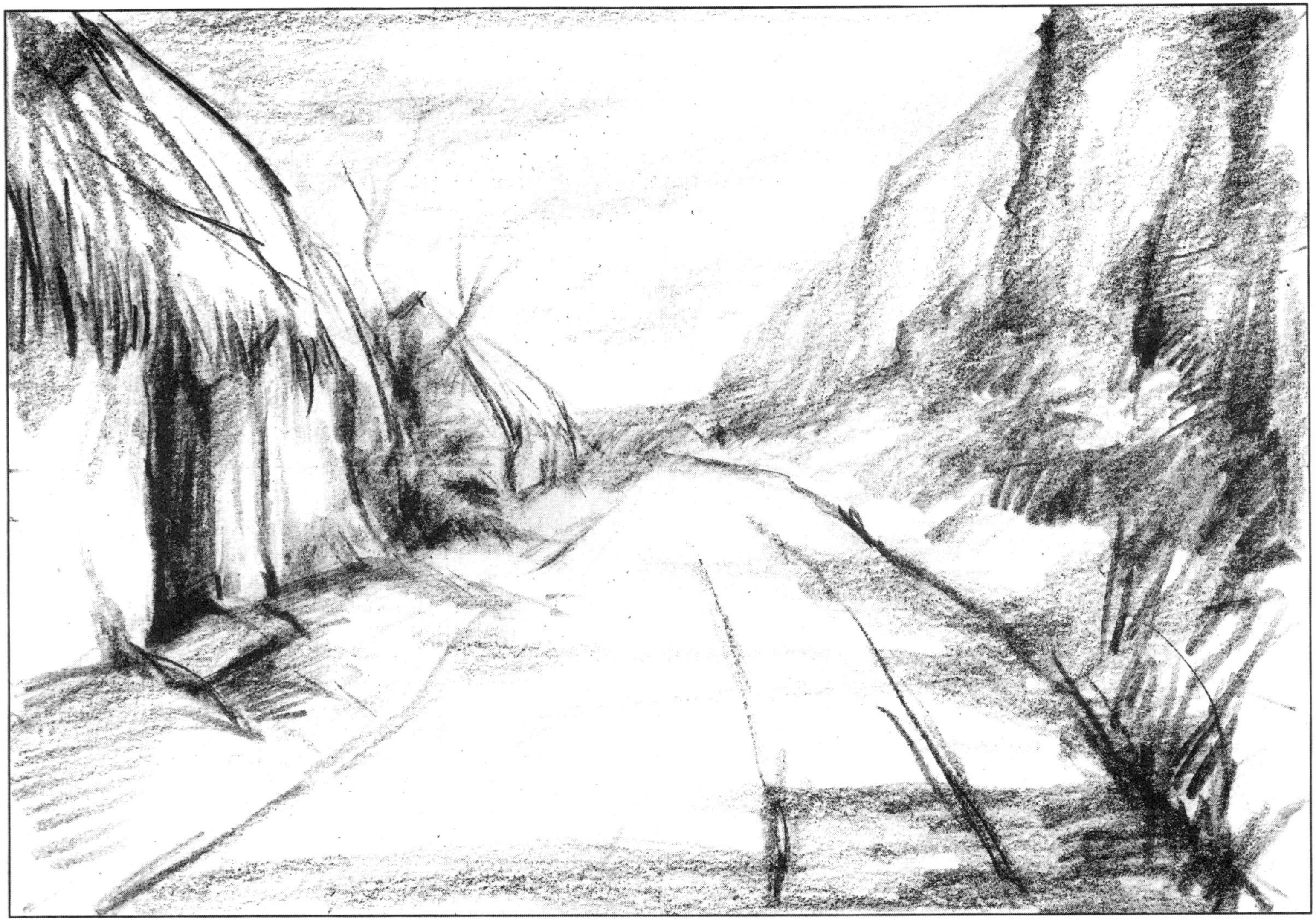

Firstly you can make a right diagram according to your calculative vanishing point. And then sketch a rough drawing over it after which you can draw the final composition.

Line & Strokes

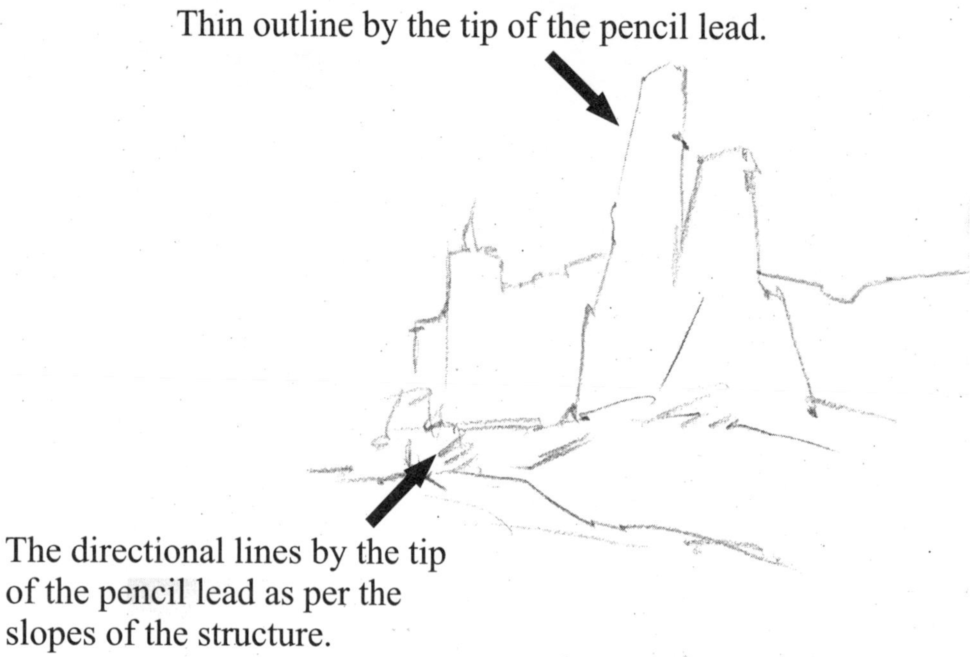

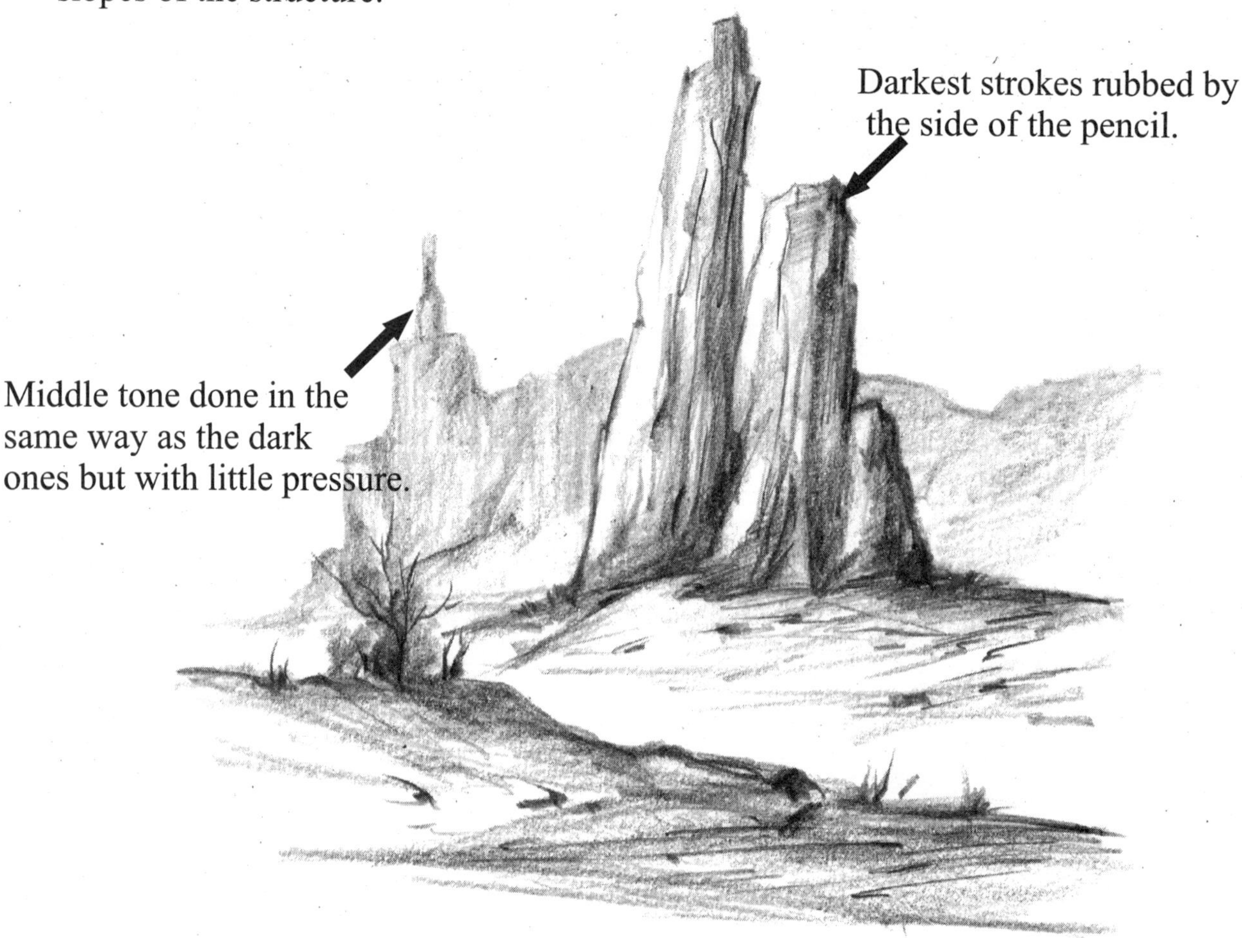

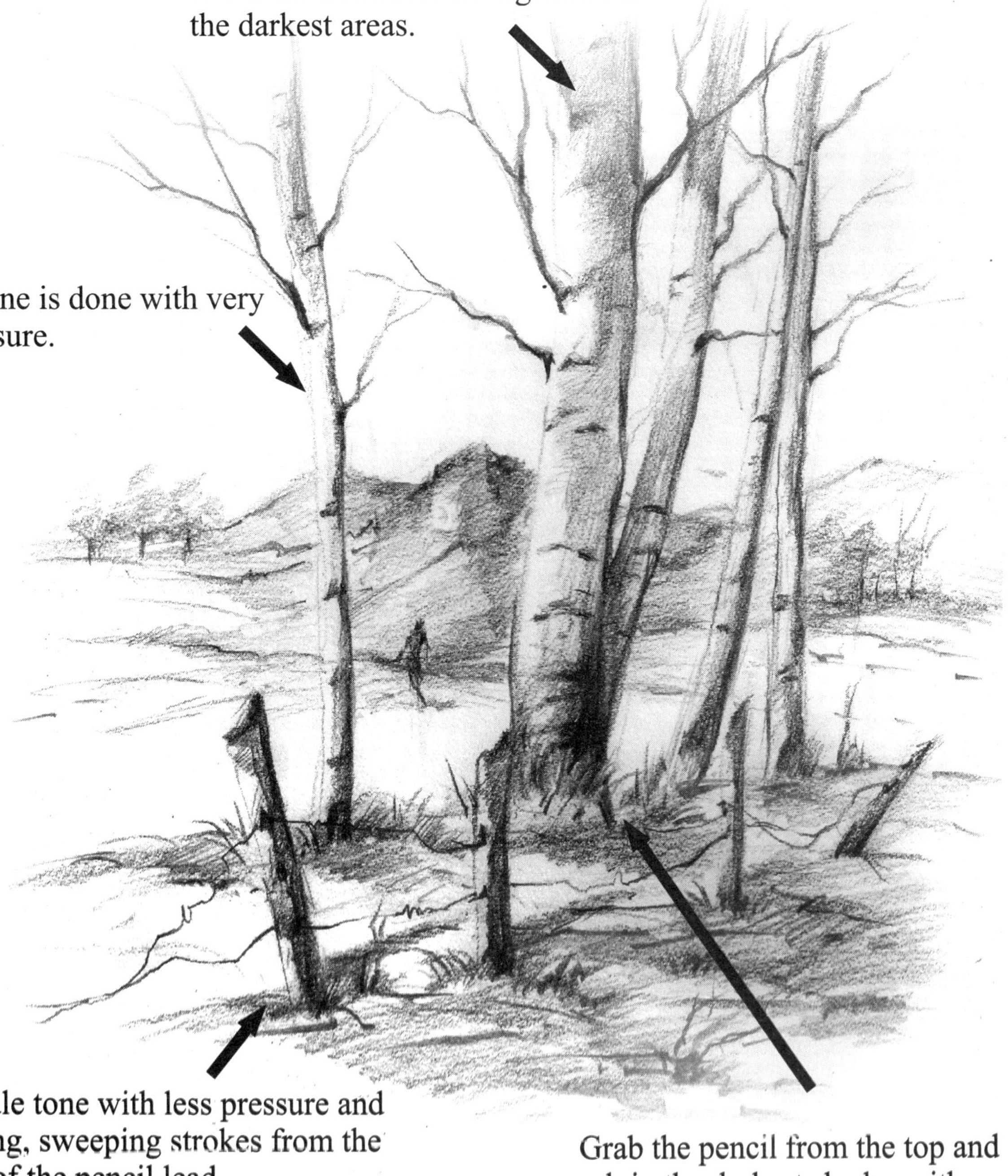
Thin and short strokes to create direction and to interconnect the lightest and the darkest areas.
Thin outline is done with very little pressure.
Middle tone with less pressure and in long, sweeping strokes from the side of the pencil lead.
Grab the pencil from the top and rub in the darkest shades with hard Pressure.

Tree & Water

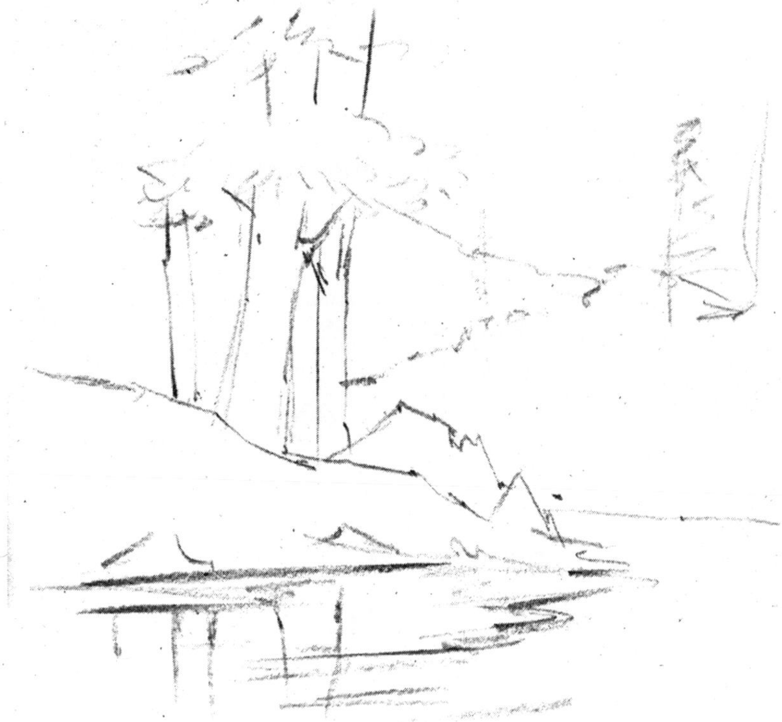

In this picture we will discuss the pencil strokes of tree and water. We will also learn the stroke perspective. Here, the tree and water are main subjects. Mountains' and distance trees' strokes have been drawn just by putting pressure on the pencil, but in case of tree and water there is a difference in the pencil stroke's dimension and depth.

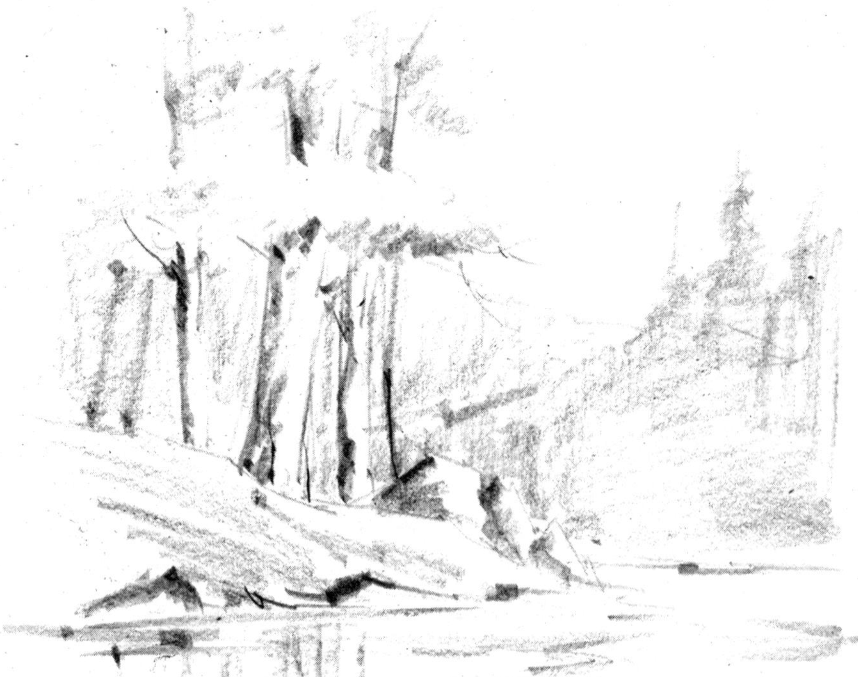

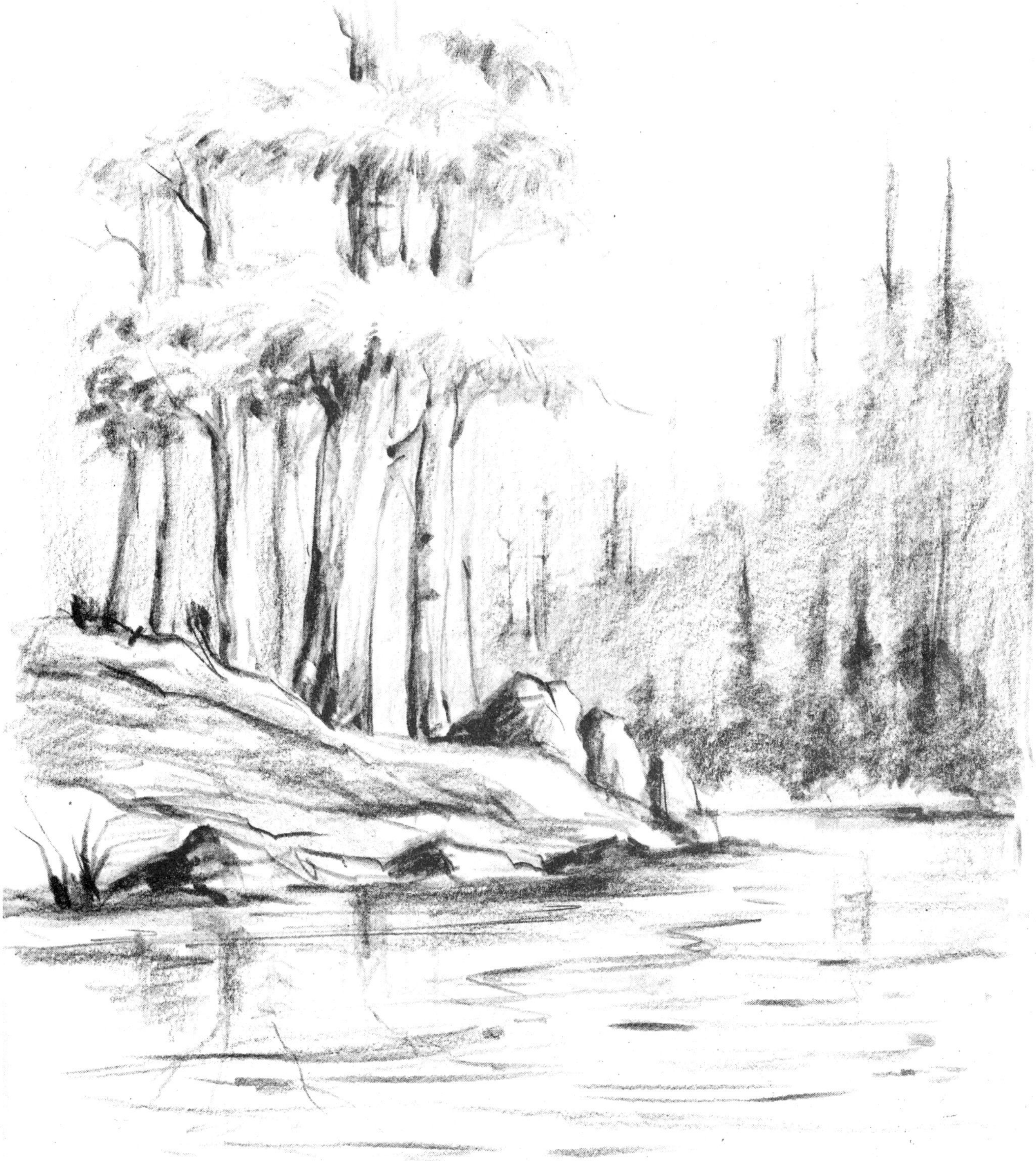

Tree

It is an essential part of any landscape. The pencil strokes change according to the character of the tree. Also, the basic light and shade is dependent on it. The step-by-step pencil strokes, pressure and direction should change accordingly. In this picture tree's and mountain's strokes should have an individual variation

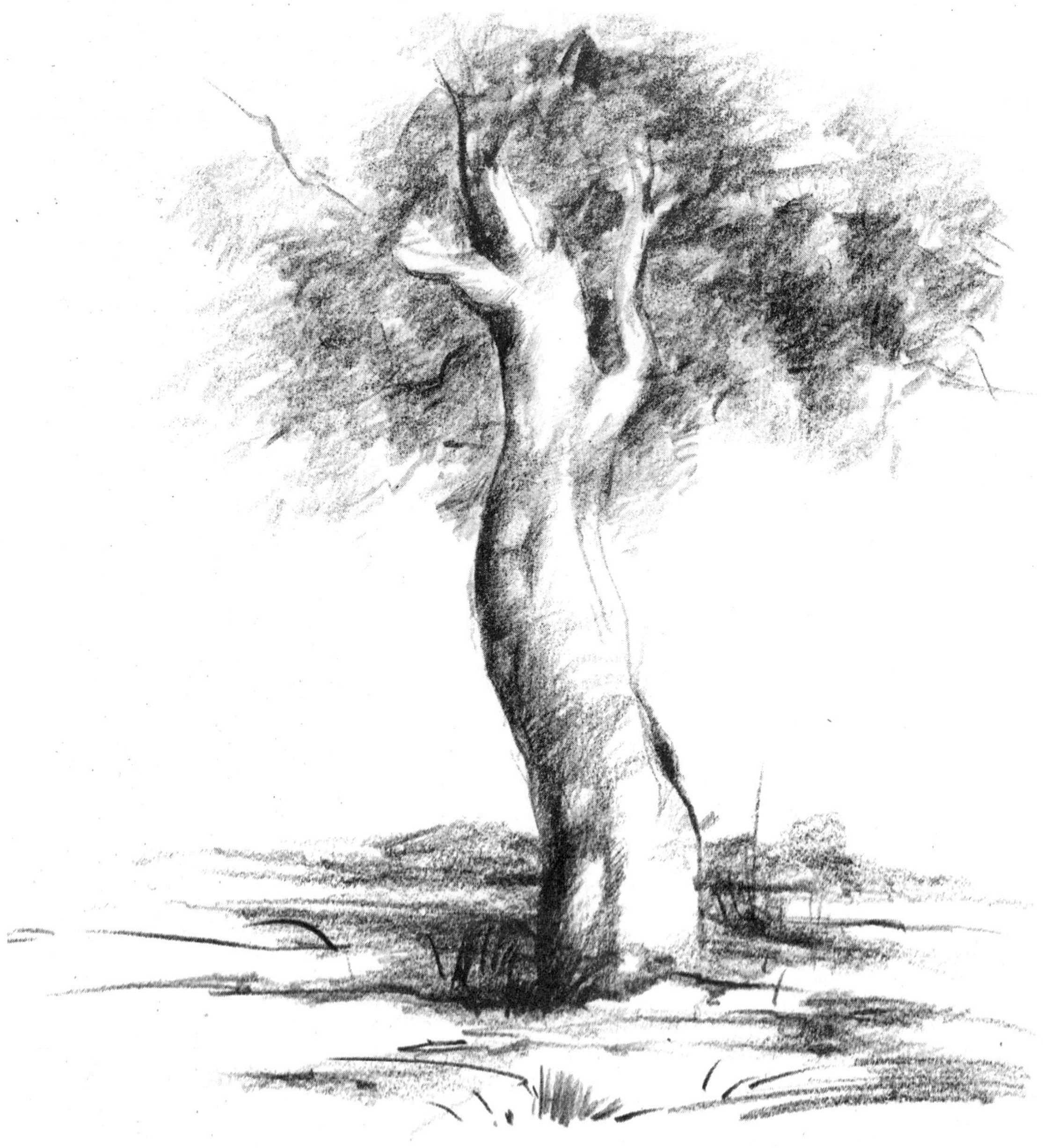

Mountain

In this picture the pencil stroke of the mountain and sky is the most important. For creating the sky a special technique has been used. In the first step, pencil stroke has been used on minimal bases and in the second step eraser has been used in some places. But for mountain, light and dark stroke has been used step by step where the function of the source of light is very important.

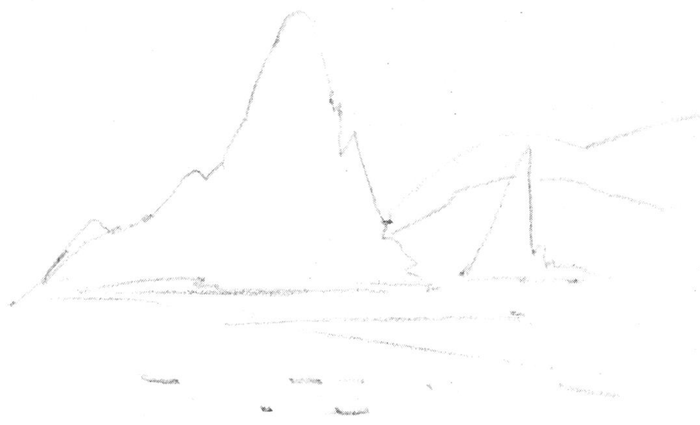

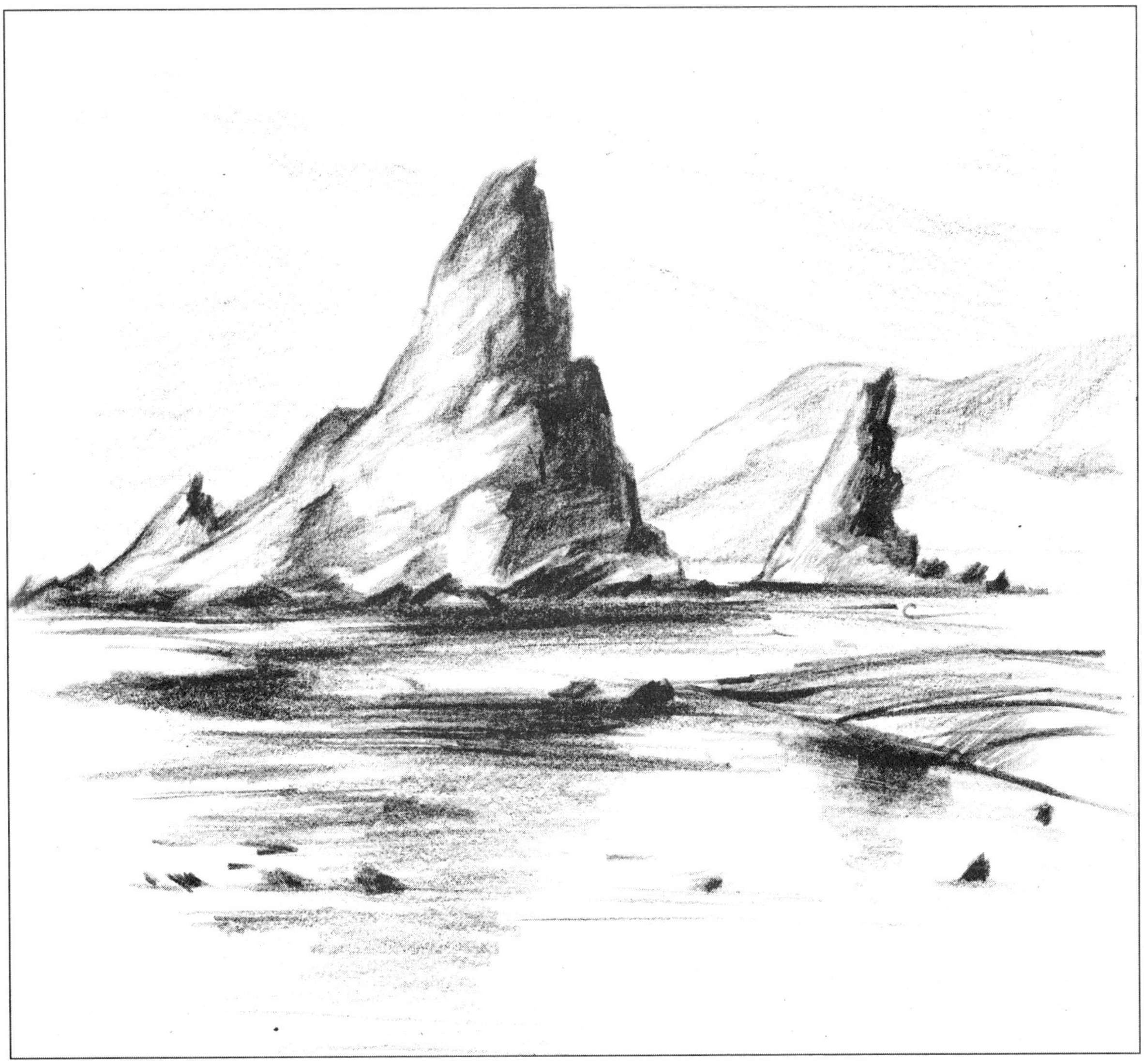

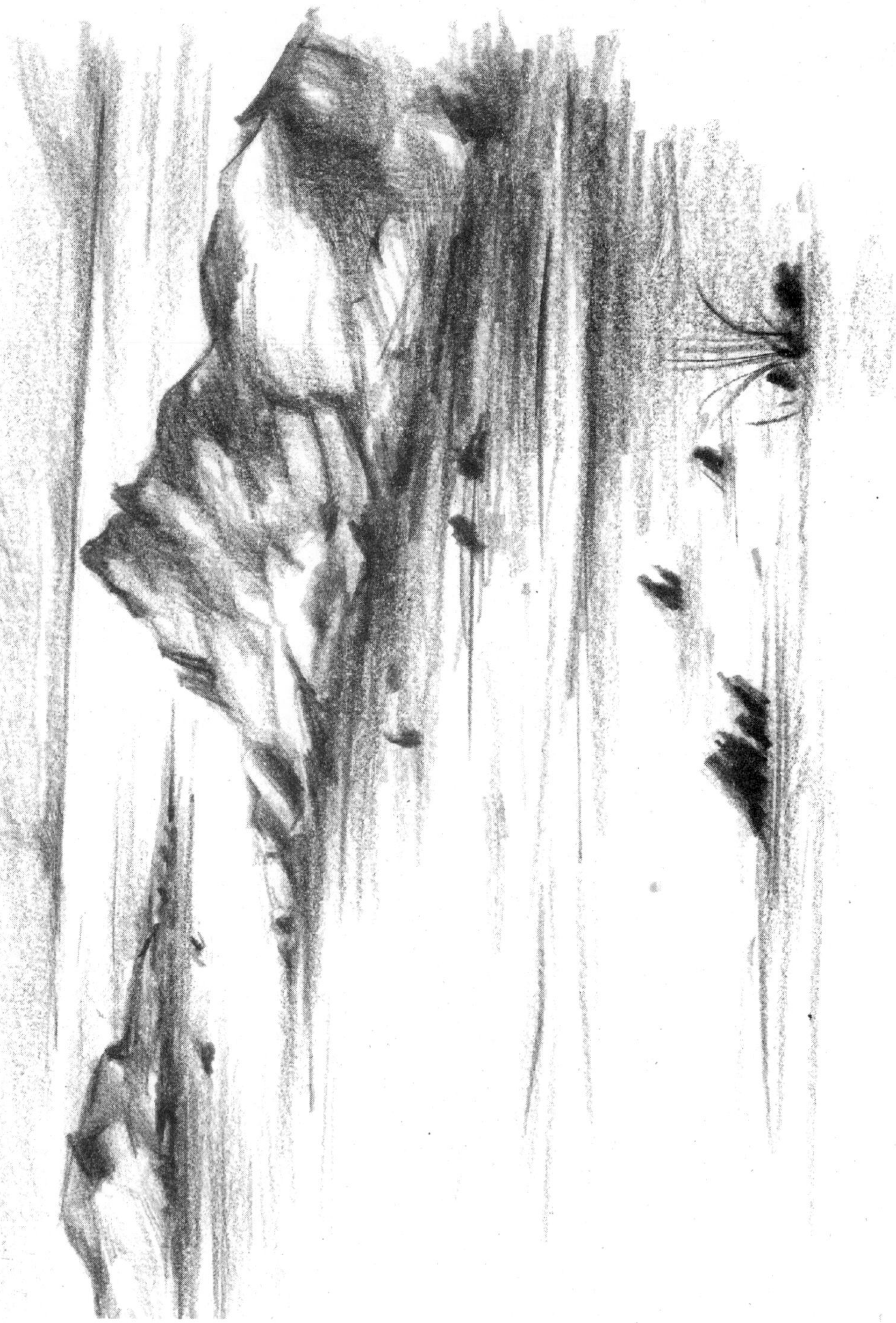

How to Start Drawing

In this picture the difference between land and mountain has been shown. Here the pencil stroke of land is very light, and for mountains according to their dimension the pencil strokes and pencil pressure has been used differently. But, in case of land, to make its dimension clear, both pencil strokes as well as paper white have been used.

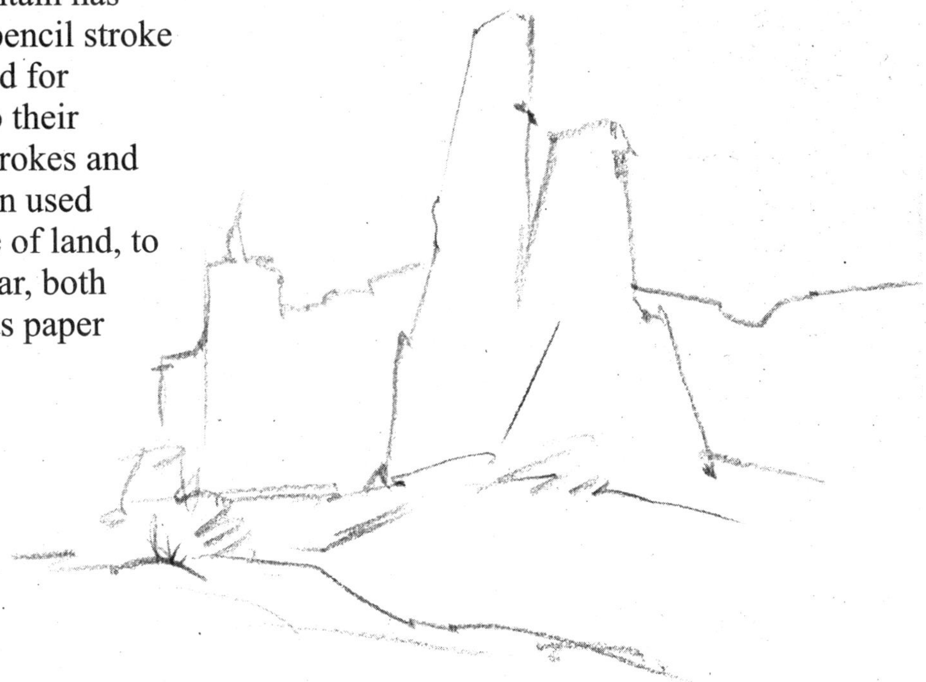

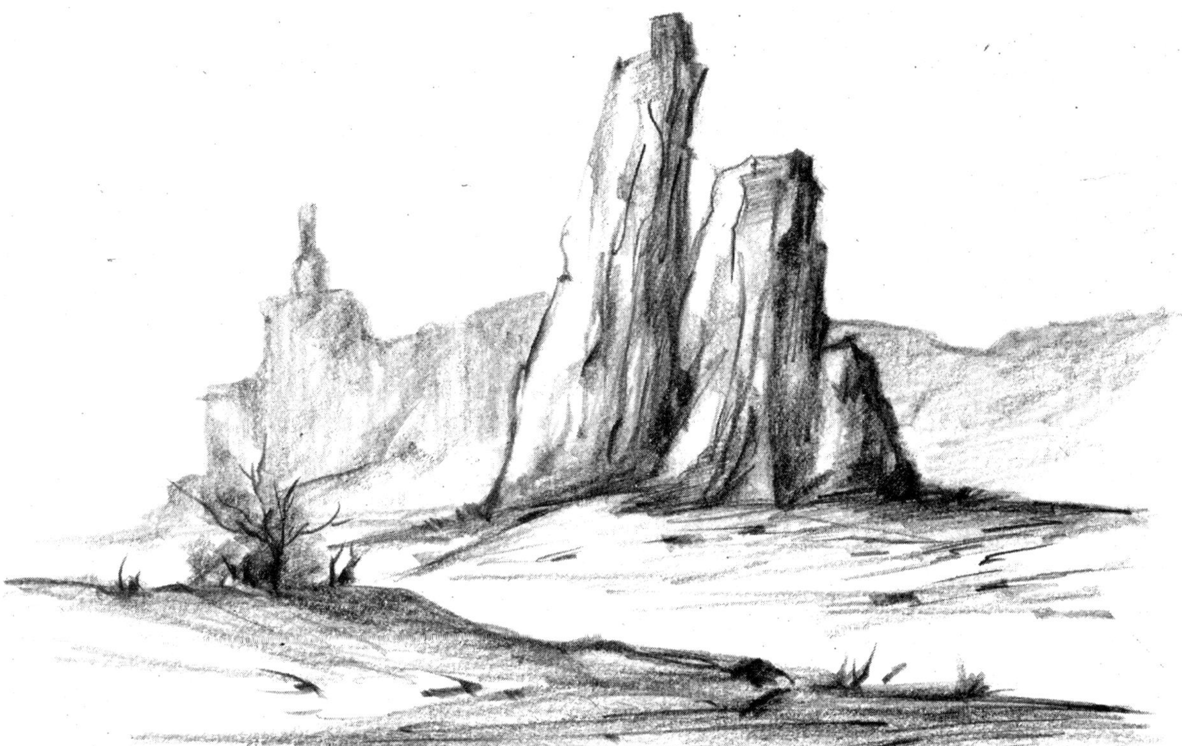

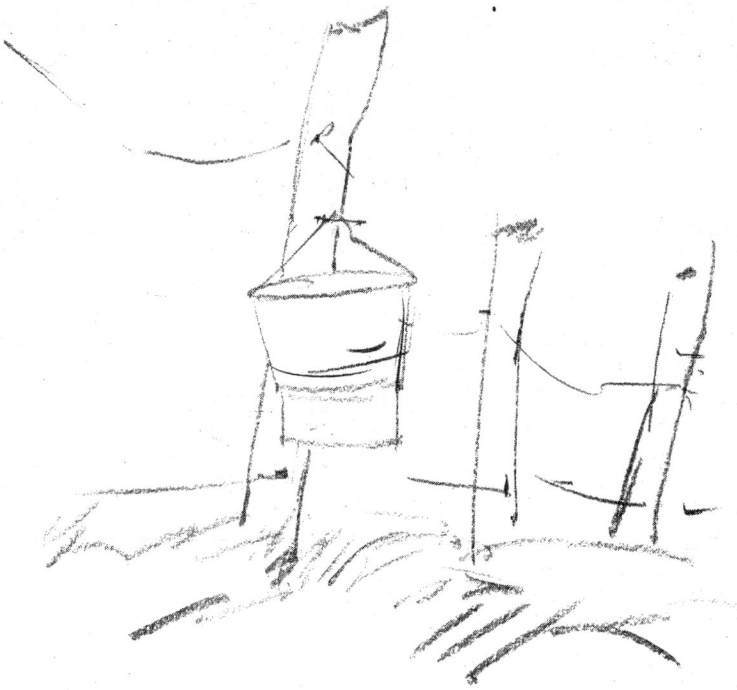

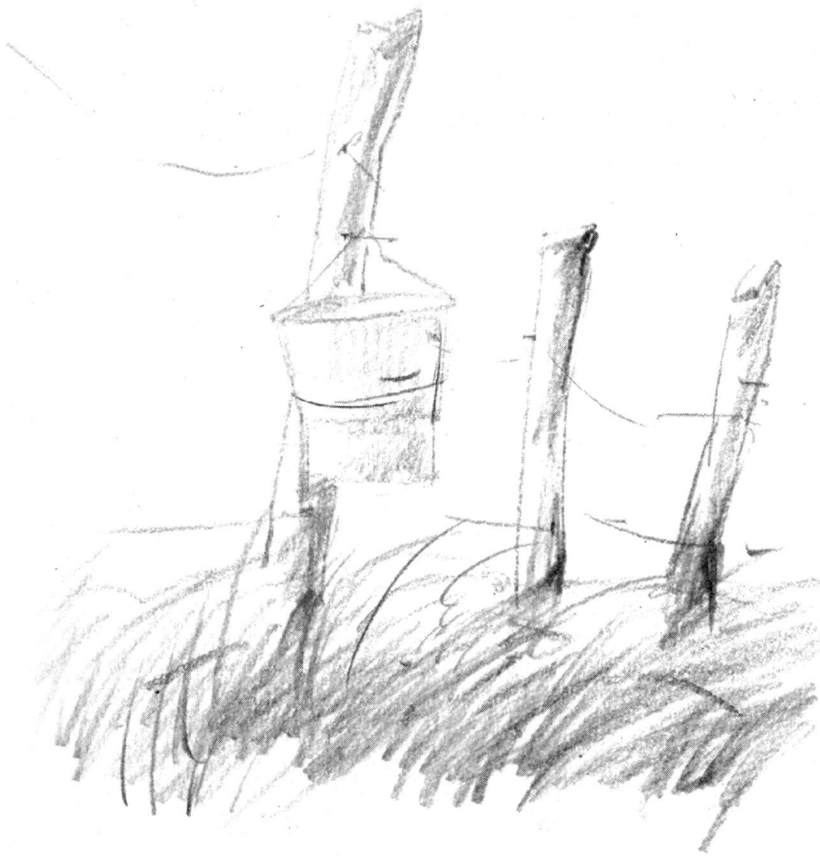

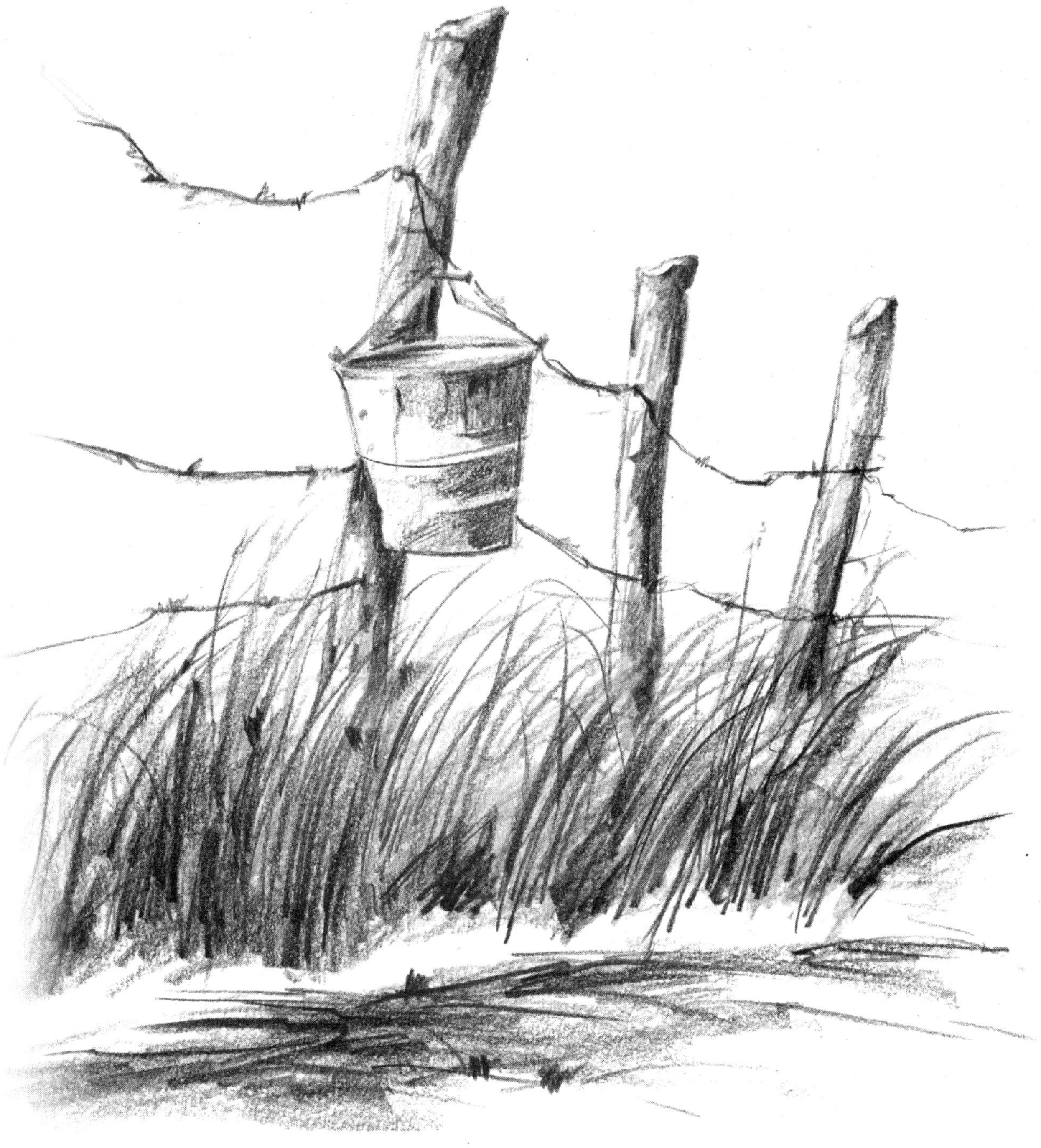

Texture and the curvatures of a certain part changes with the view and you should be able to capture that difference.

Mountain and Hut

We should learn the difference between the strokes used in mountain and hut as there's a difference in their elements. In this picture, the dimension of source of light has been handled softly. After this, in case of mountain the stroke direction has been used in a bold manner. But in case of hut, the stroke direction and dimension is used lightly, also the stroke direction is vertical.

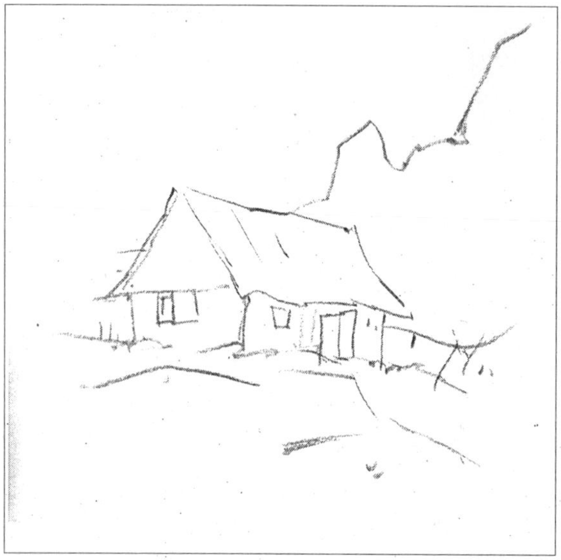

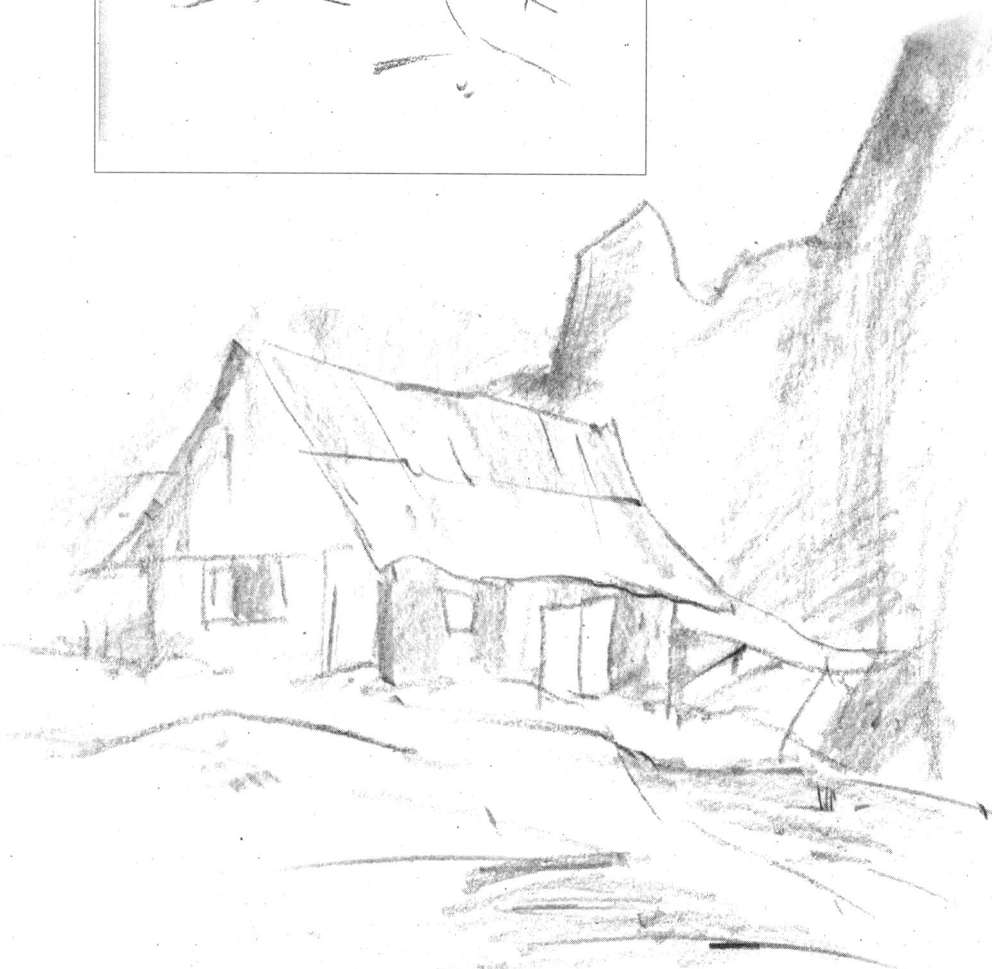

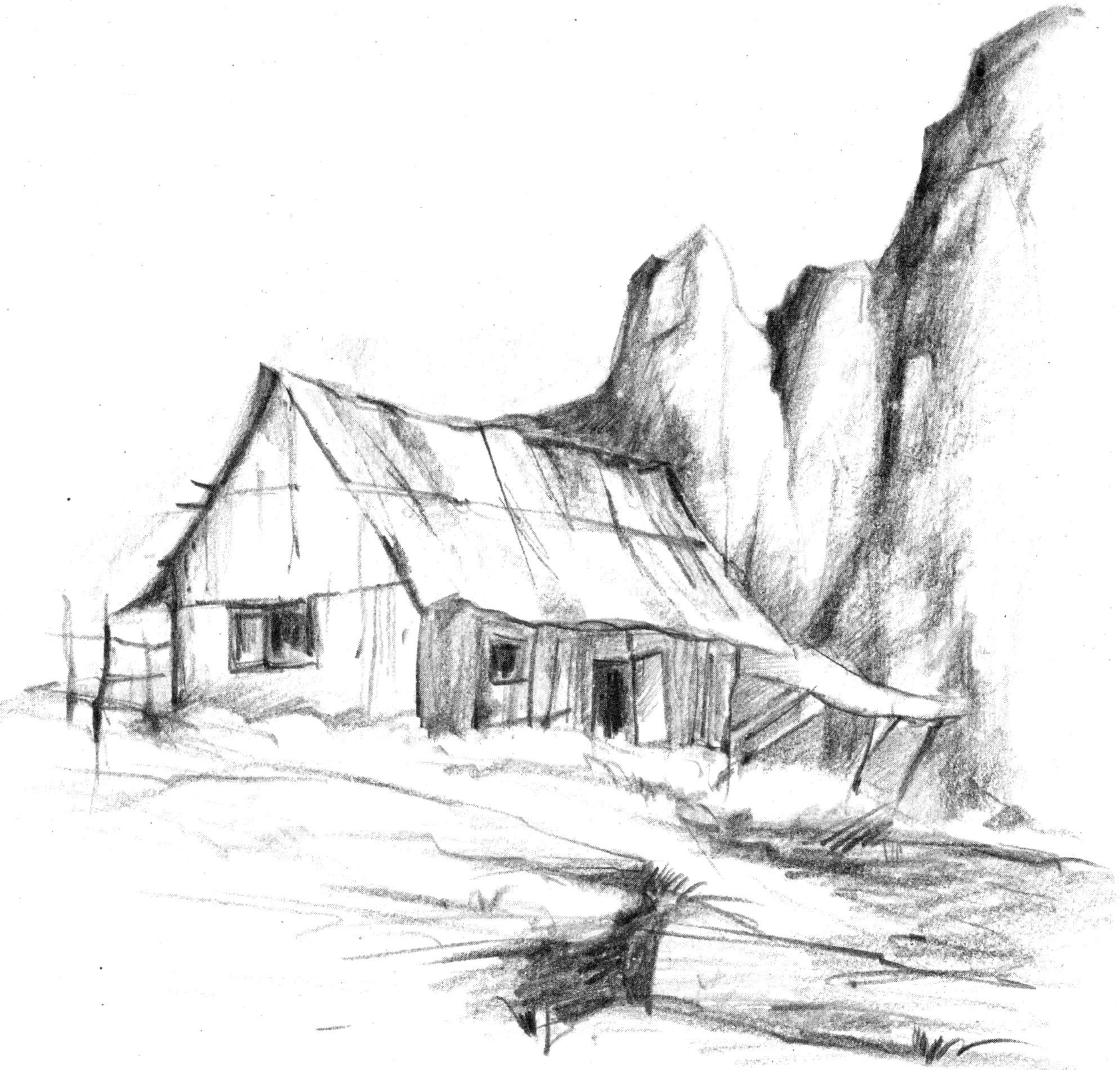

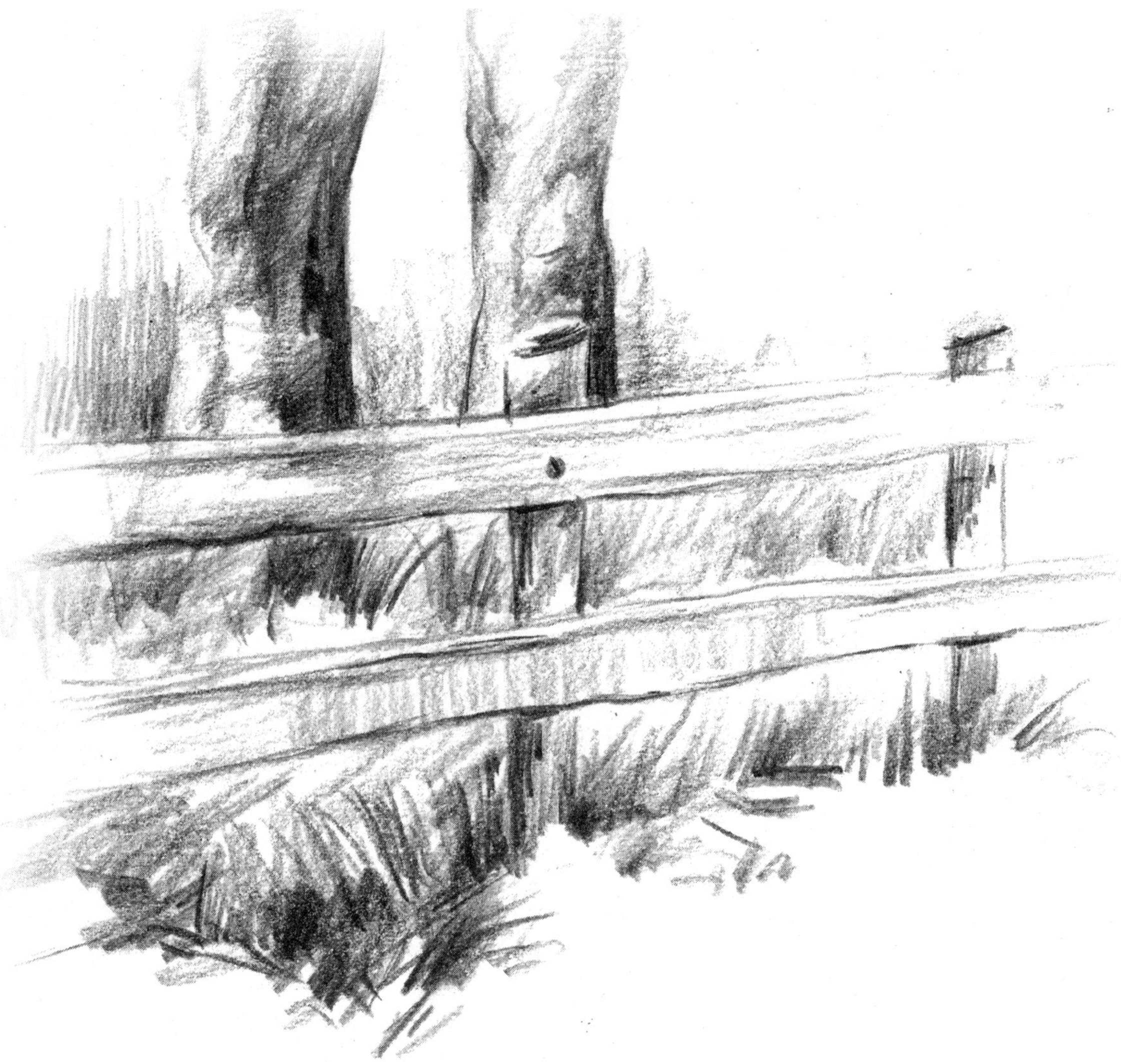

Fence

In this picture the drawing of the fence and the placement of stroke has been shown, we should also observe the direction of the grass. In landscape the character of the stroke is different because the character of the light source is different.

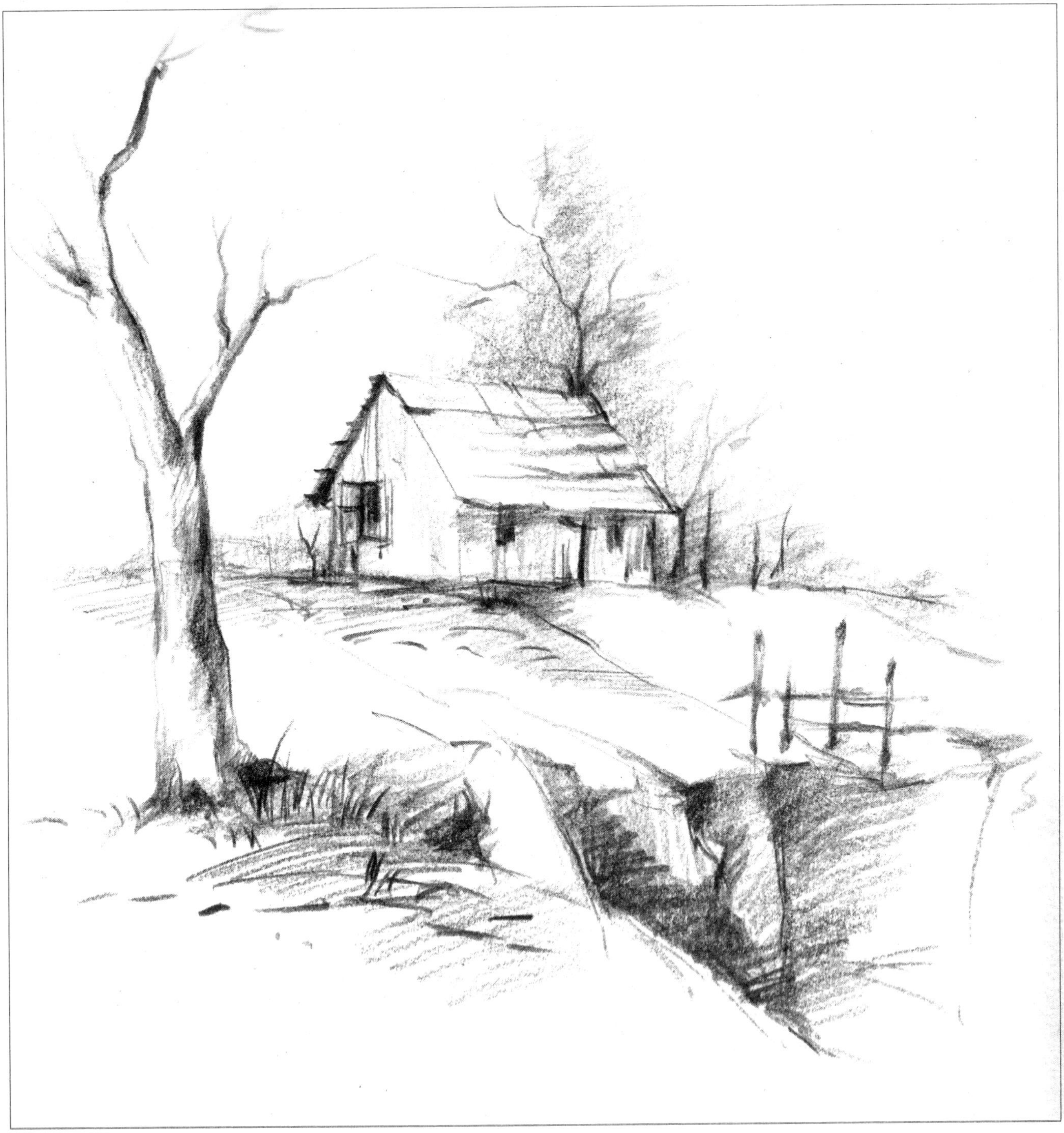

Rainy day

In landscape the use of stroke is very much different when we show a rainy day. The pencil pressure is used lightly, also according to it we should show the dimension and the detailing of the subject. To show rain drops we can use straight lines in the drawing.

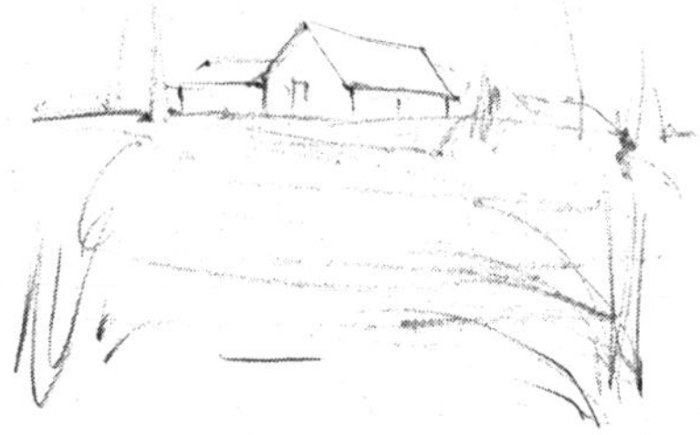

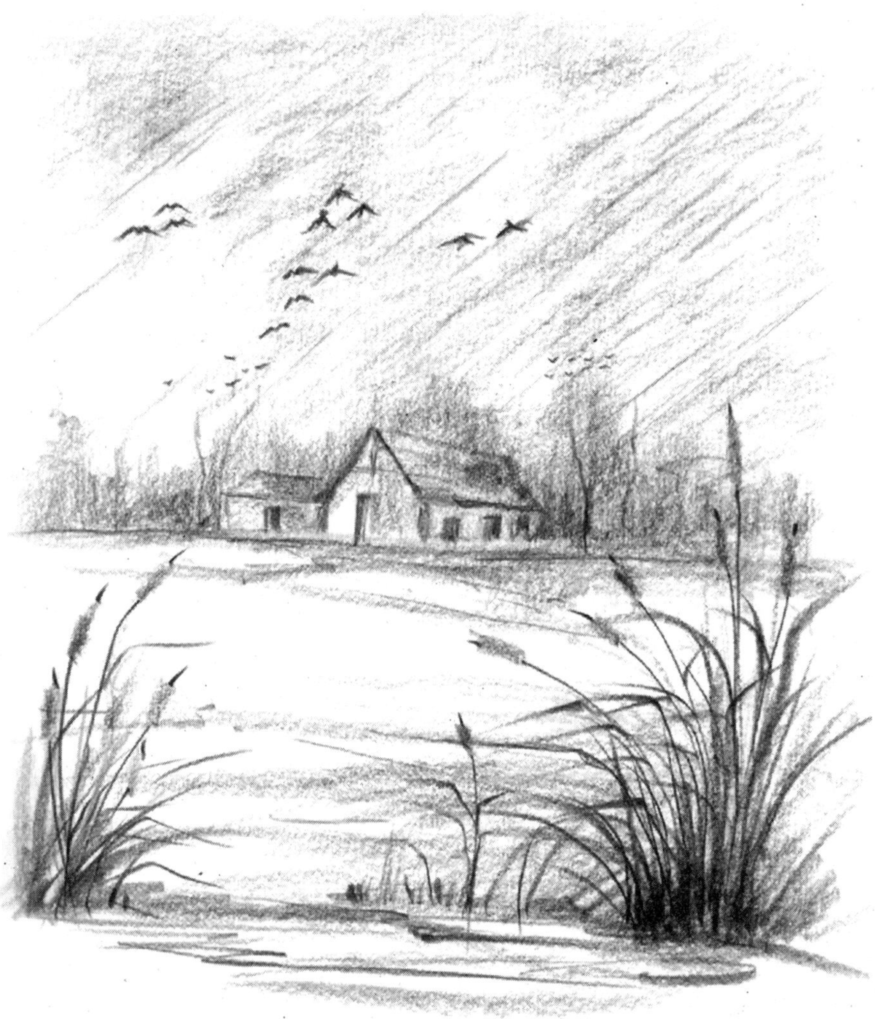

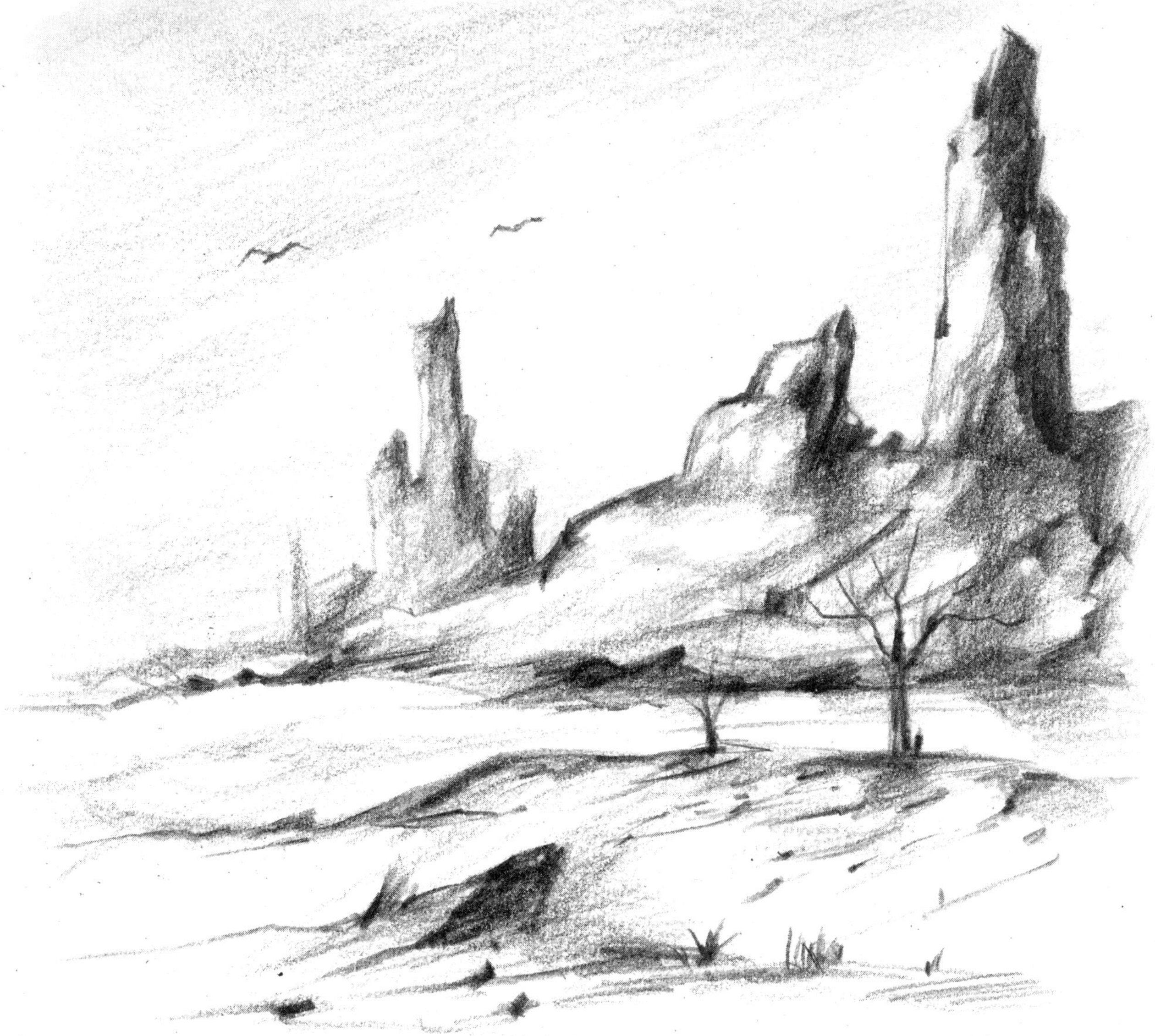

Once you got control on your pencil then the lines are like a melody. You can play and enjoy it as and when you wish.

In this picture we have shown rainwater as well as the reflection falling on it. To understand the reflection we should also observe the subject's reflection and character. In case of reflection the strokes are used vertically.

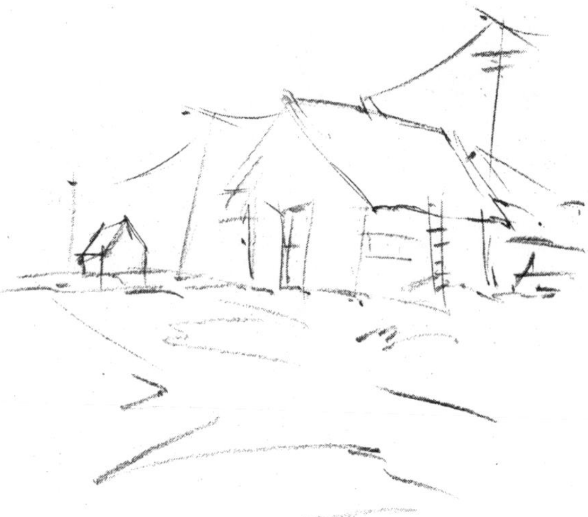

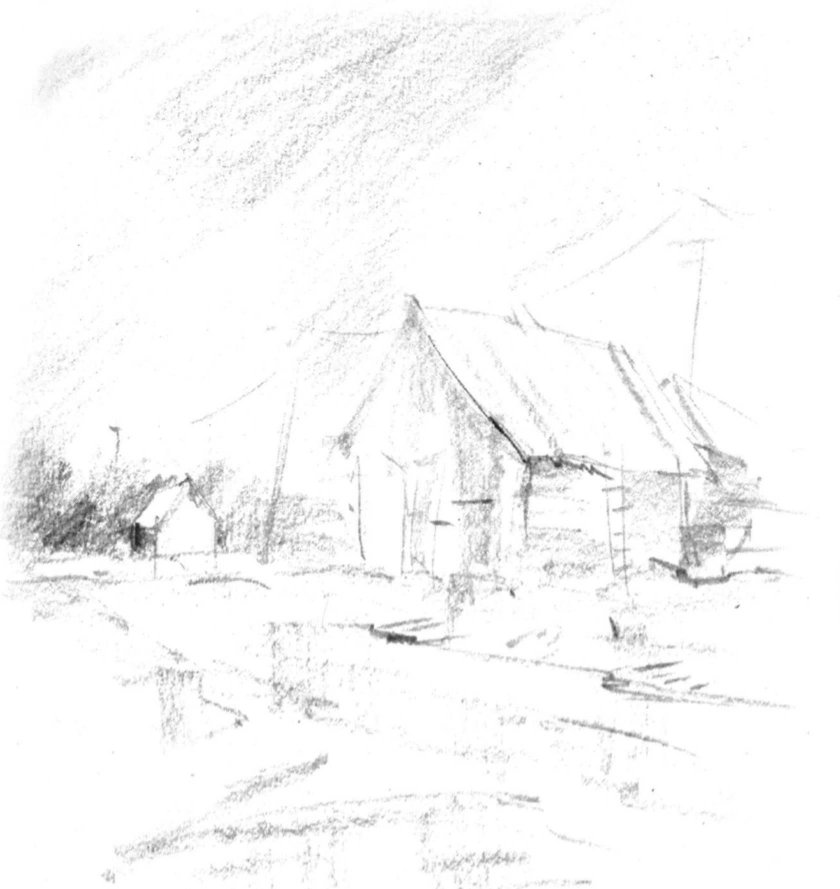

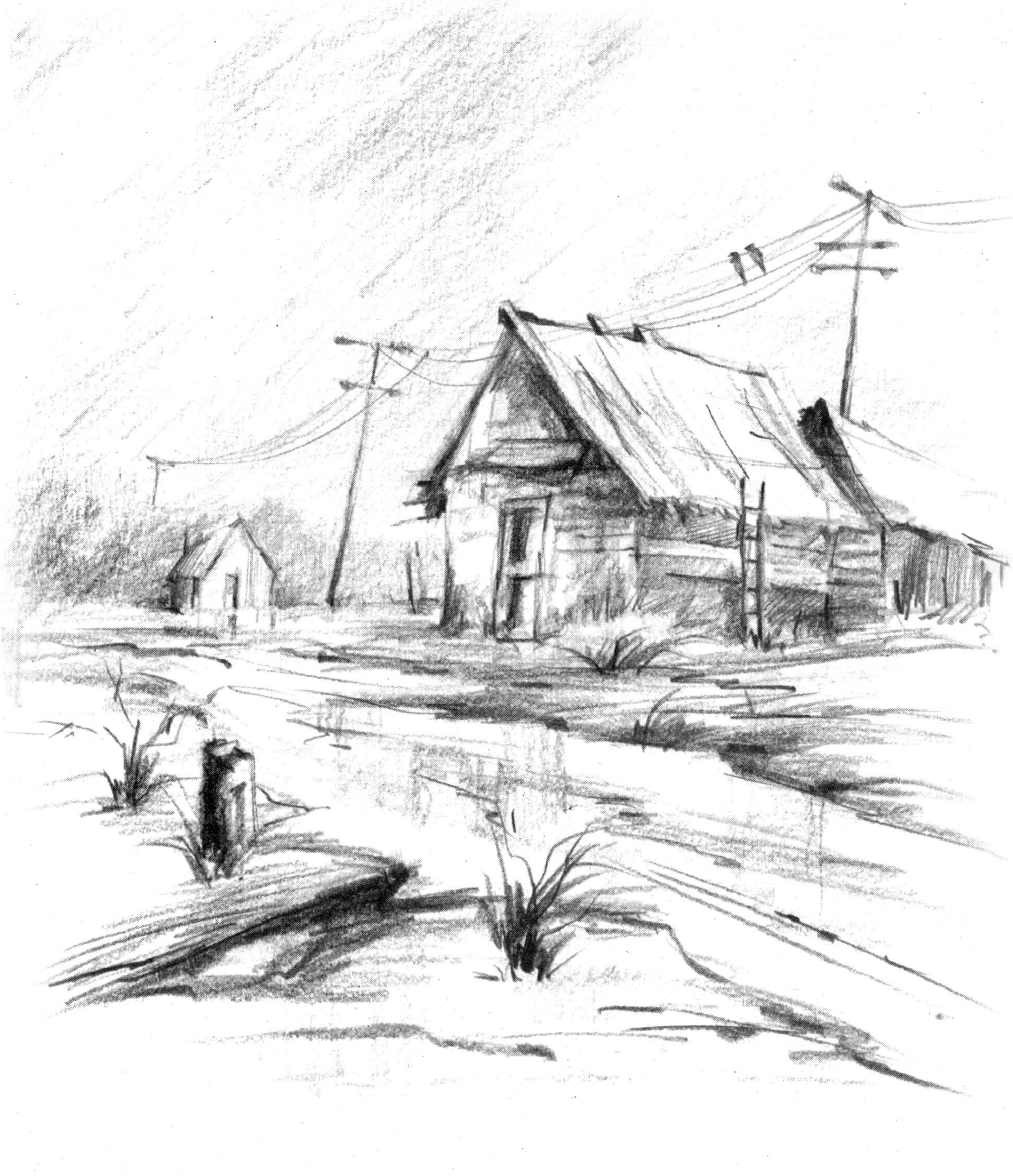

Water

Bringing out the character of water is a bit difficult in pencil stroke, as water is colourless. Water reflects the same image of any object, which is near it. By using the paper white and source of light we can show the character of water. In this picture the reflection of boat has been shown. We can also show the reflection by using the pencil stroke's pressure lightly. If used properly we can understand the variation of pencil strokes and achieve the skills.

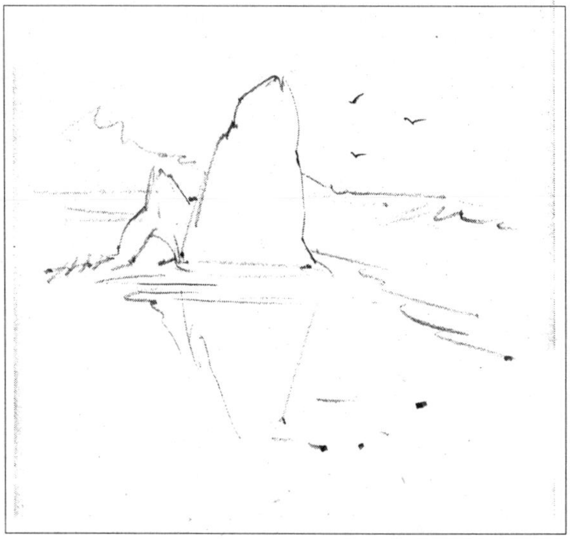

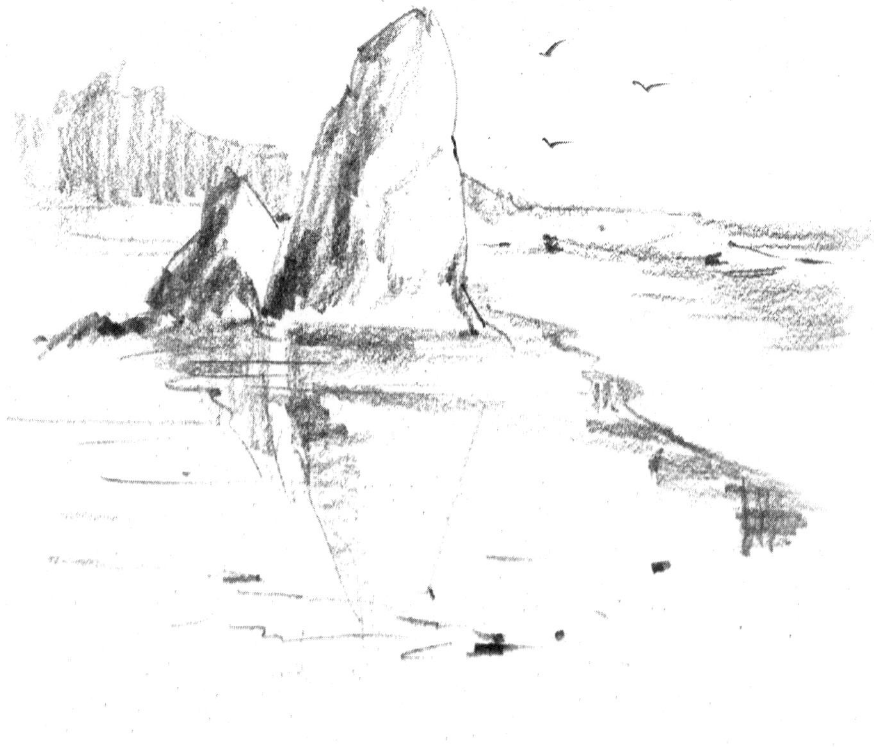

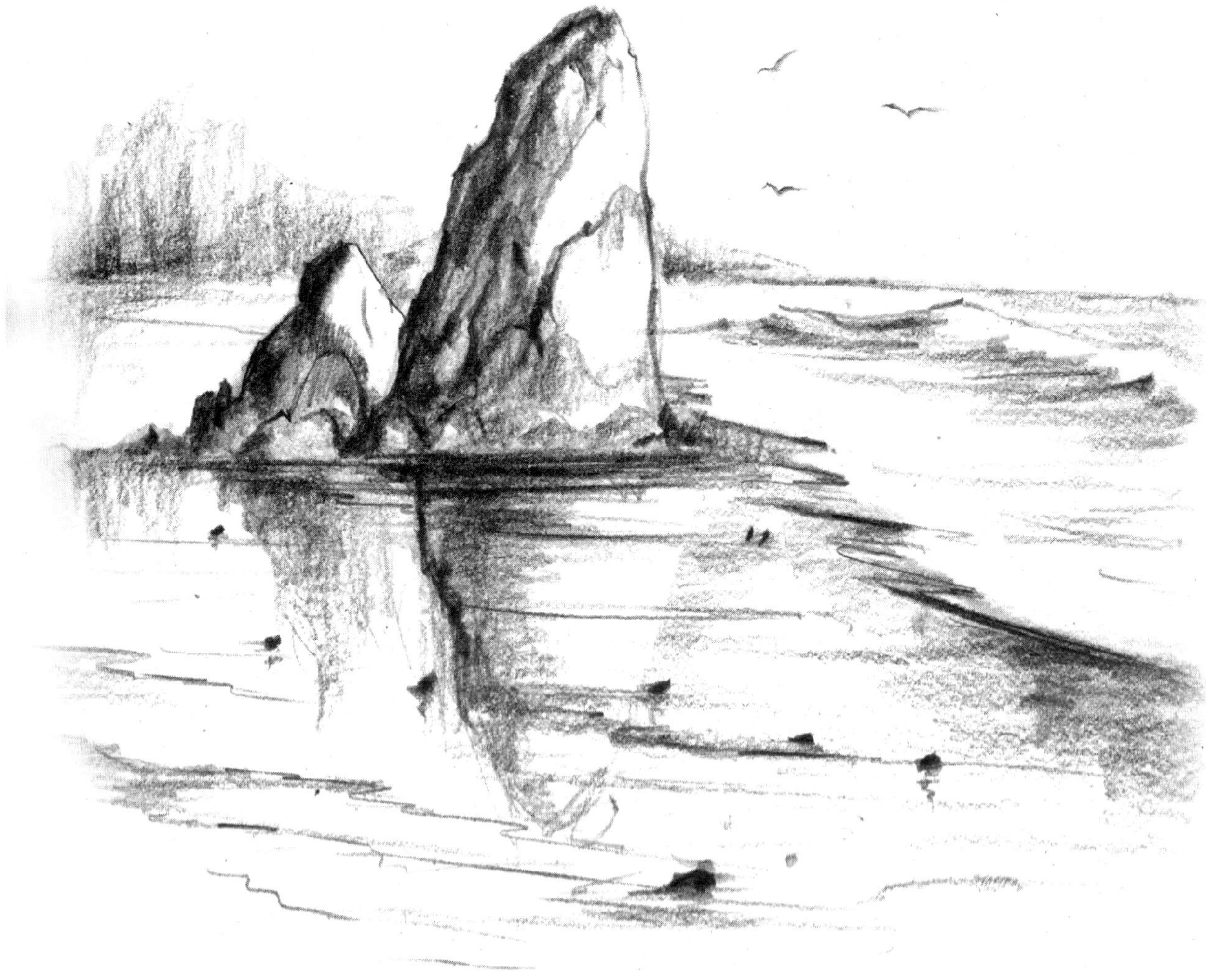

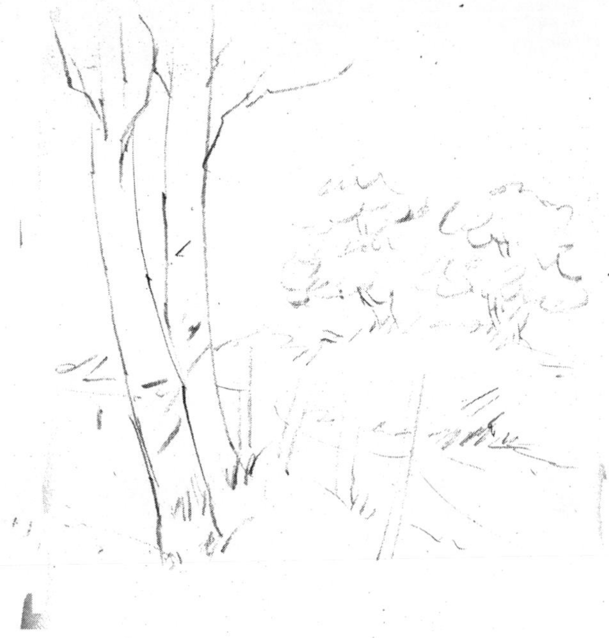

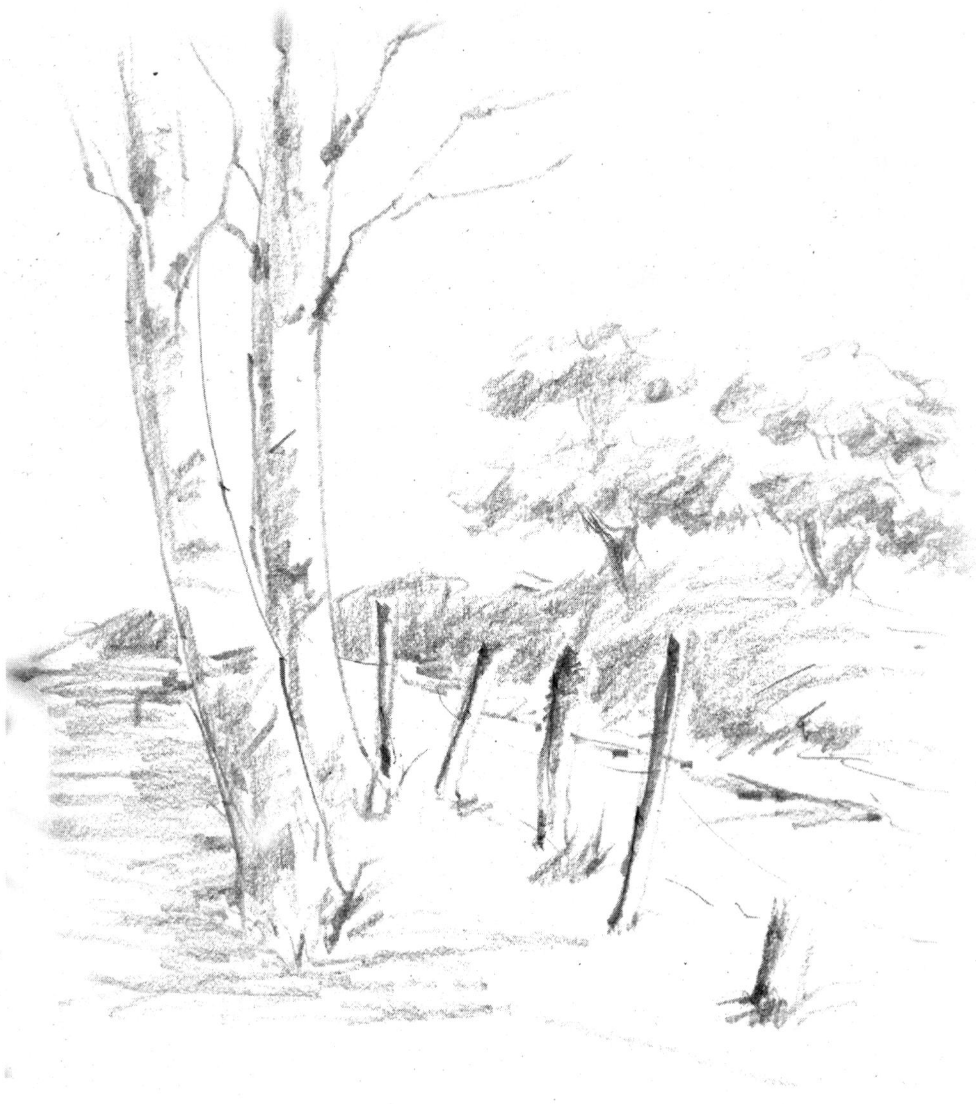

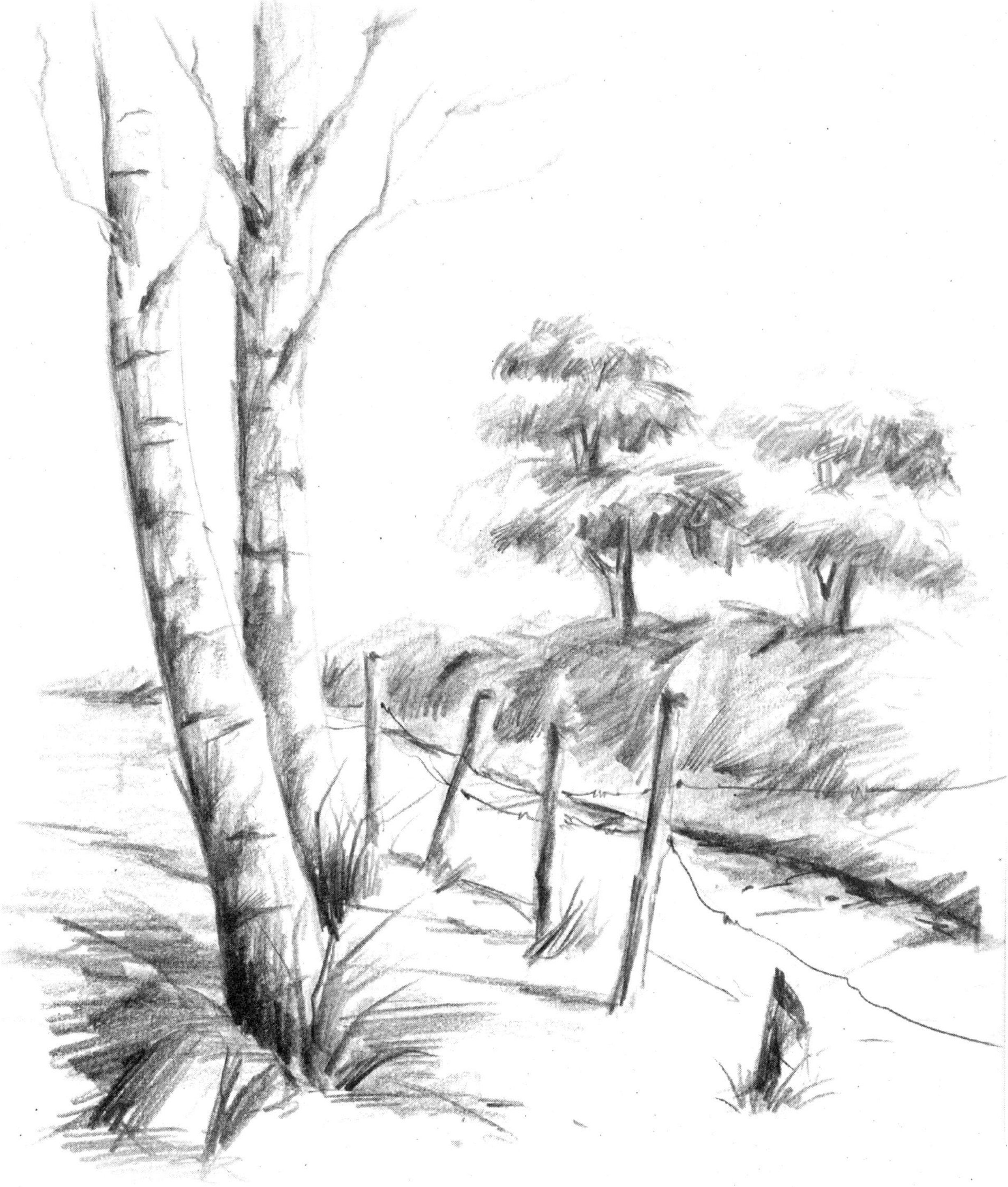

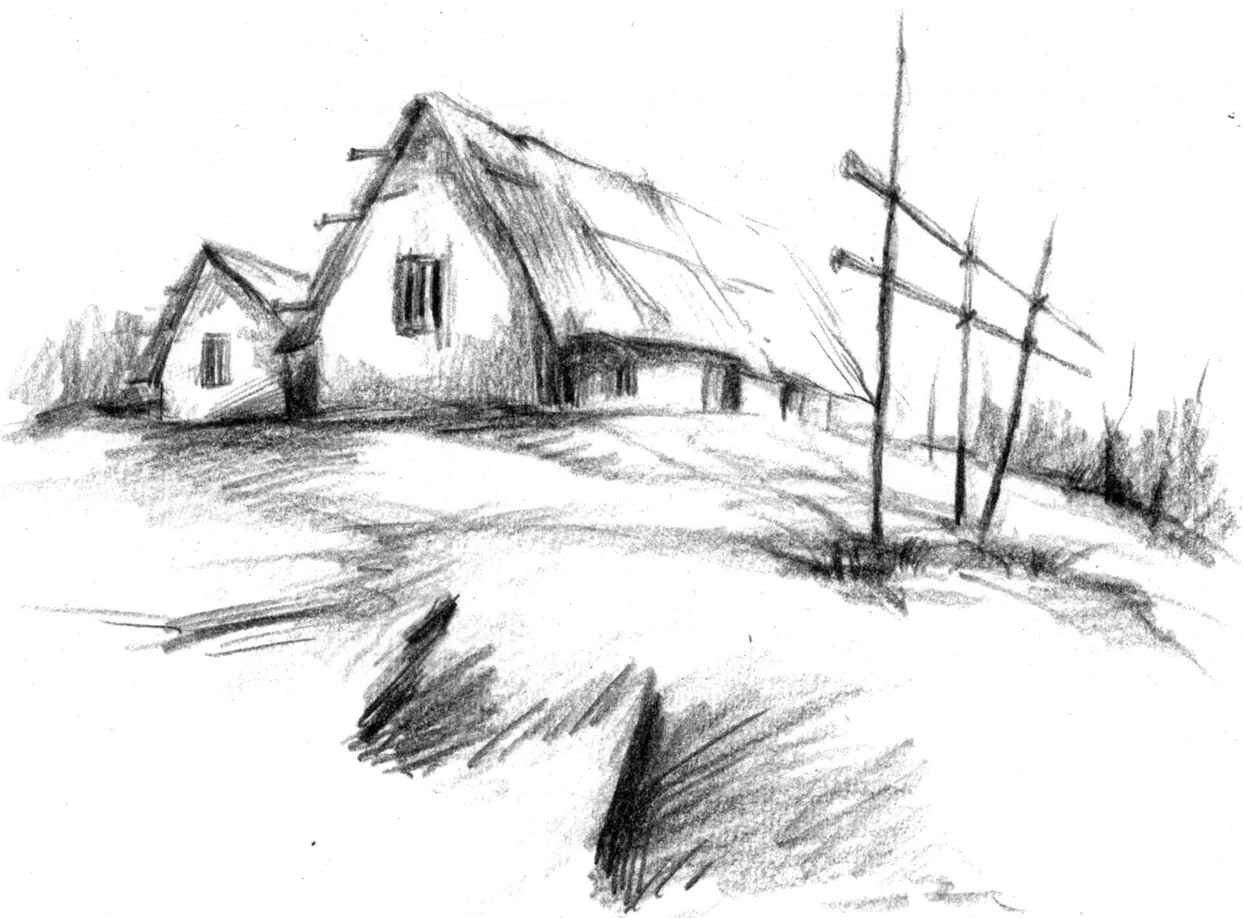

How to Finish

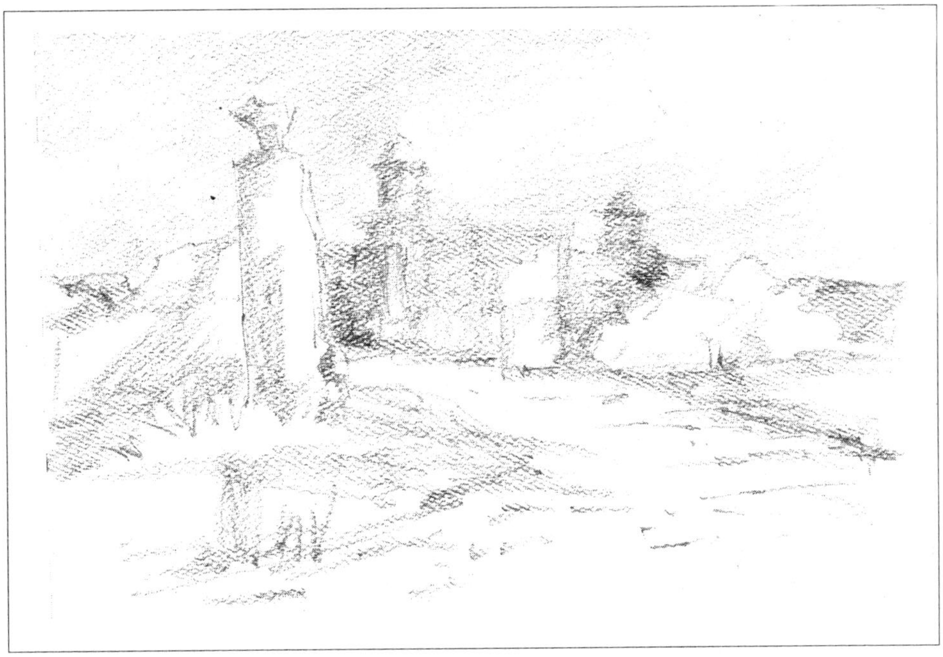

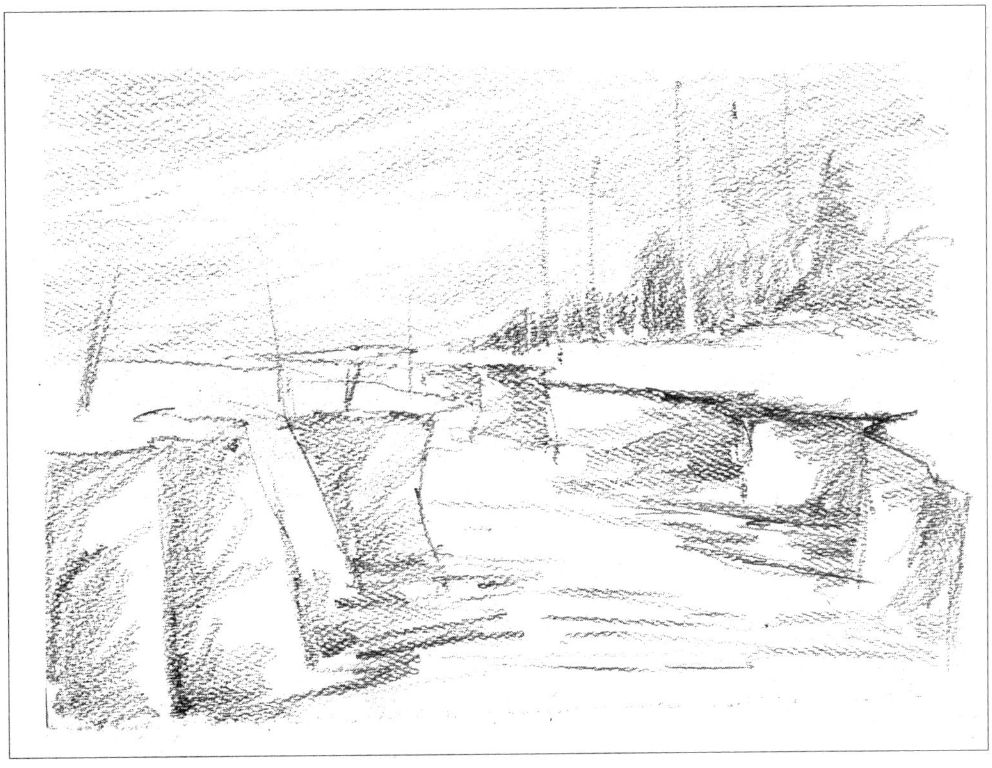

Keep coming back to the basics whenever you choose a new subject to draw. On all these pages I have tried several angles and poses to study the form. Have a close look on them and copy if you like.

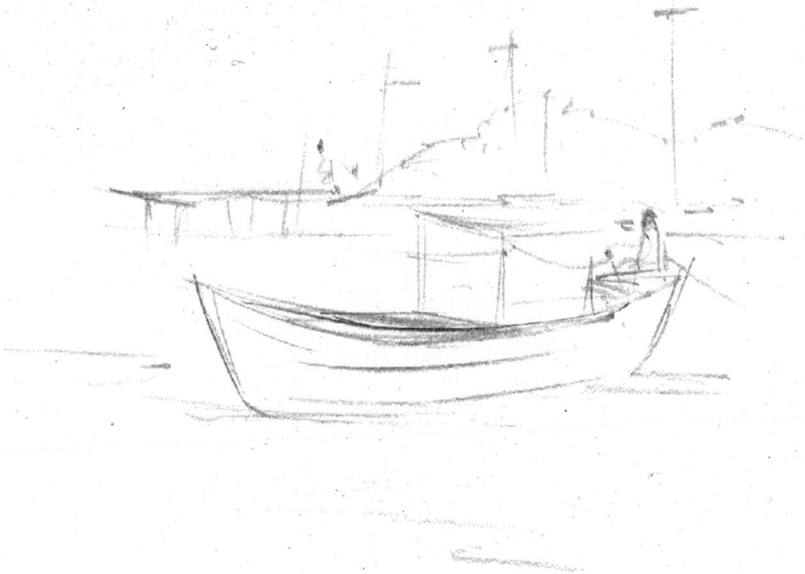

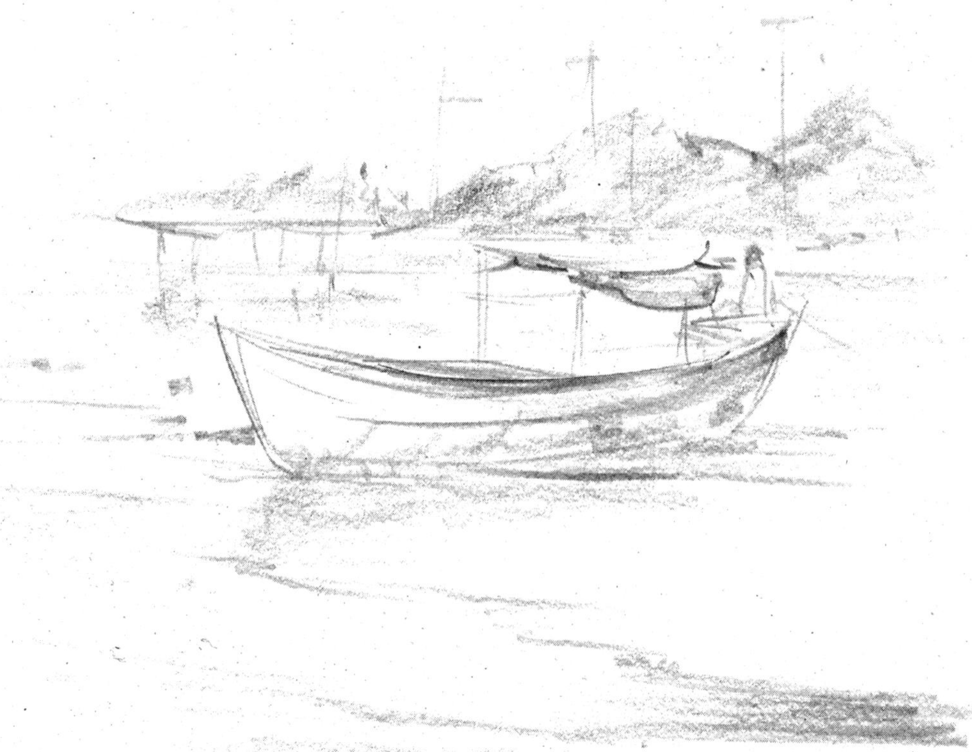

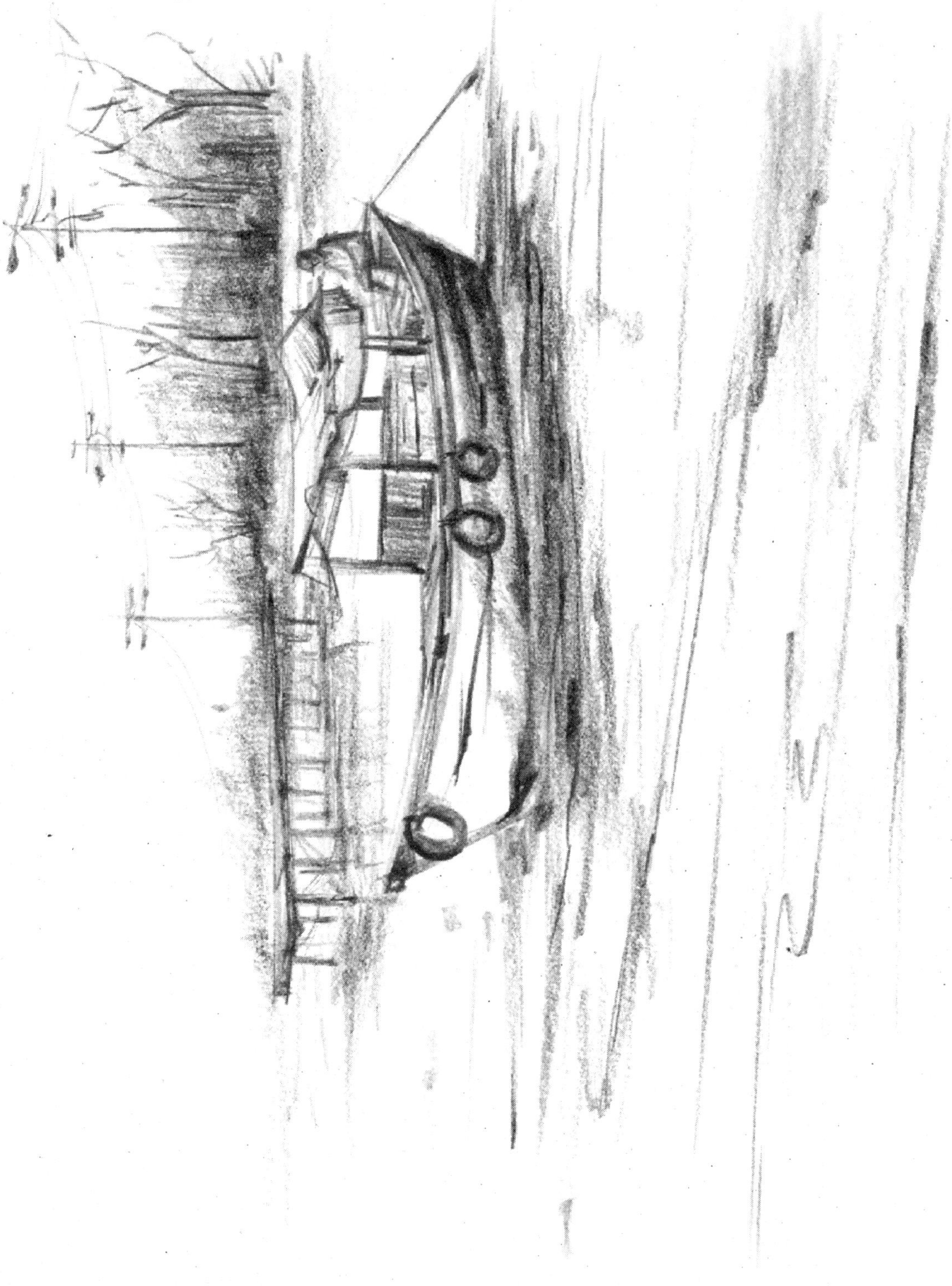

In nature, practically everything is a good subject for drawing. So draw what you like. Remember the line drawing is always important because it provides the structure, shades only create volume and planes. Another factor which become significant here is the way you define texture.

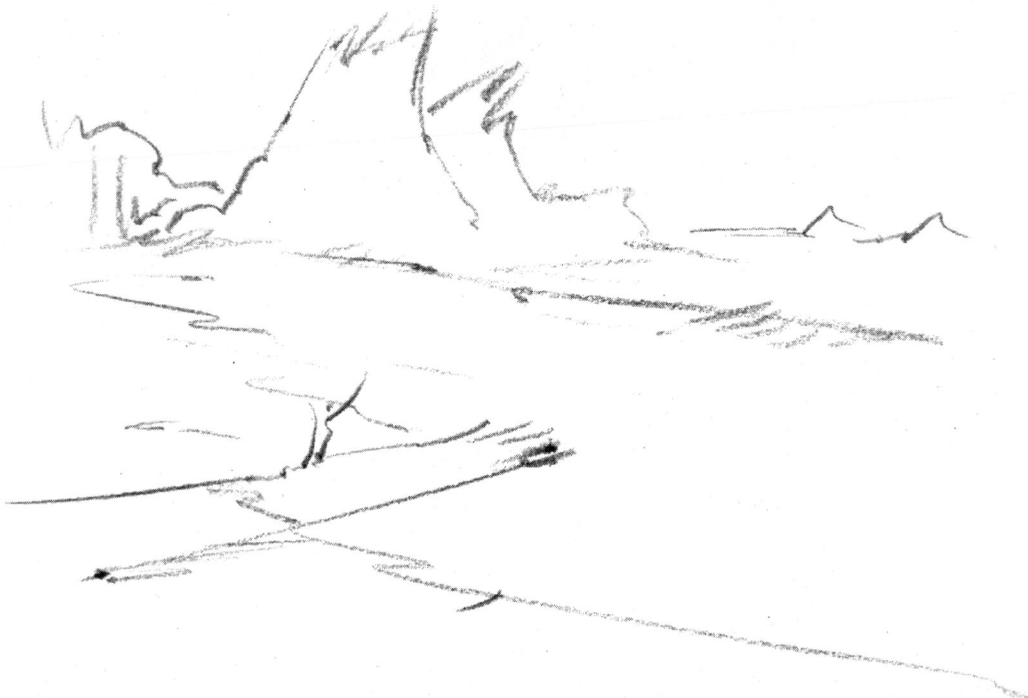

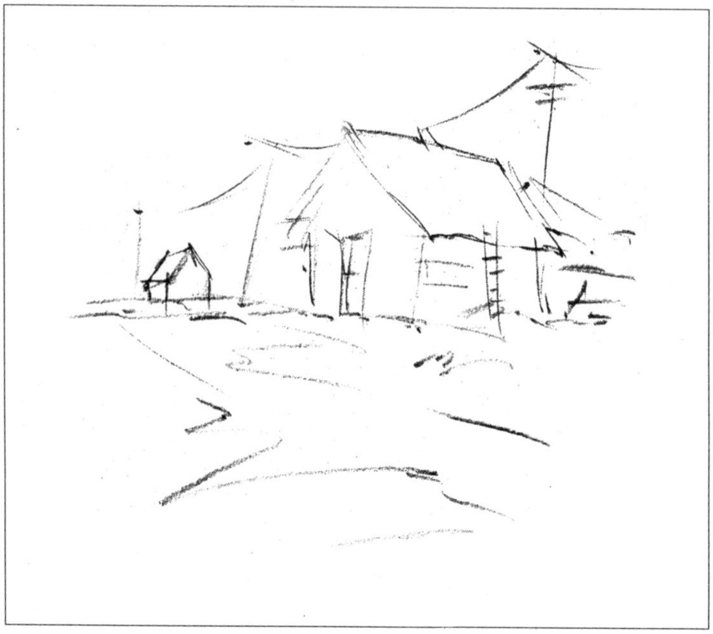

Sea and it reflection

To show sea we use a bit technicality. To show waves we can use paper white. In case of reflection the reflected element's volume as well as the surface of the subject should be understandable. To show the reflection, we should use paper white and vertical strokes.

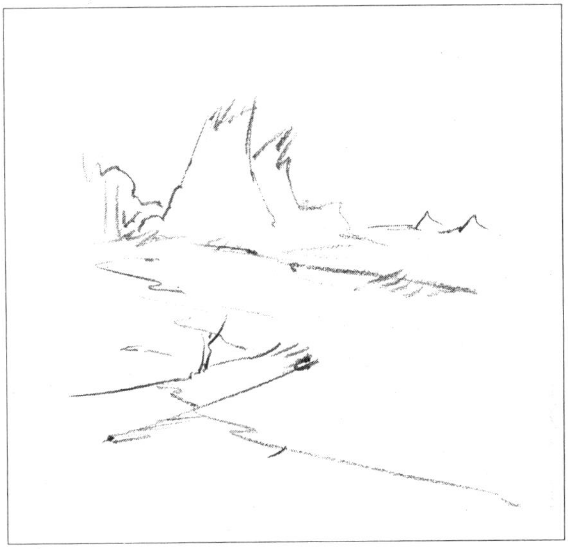

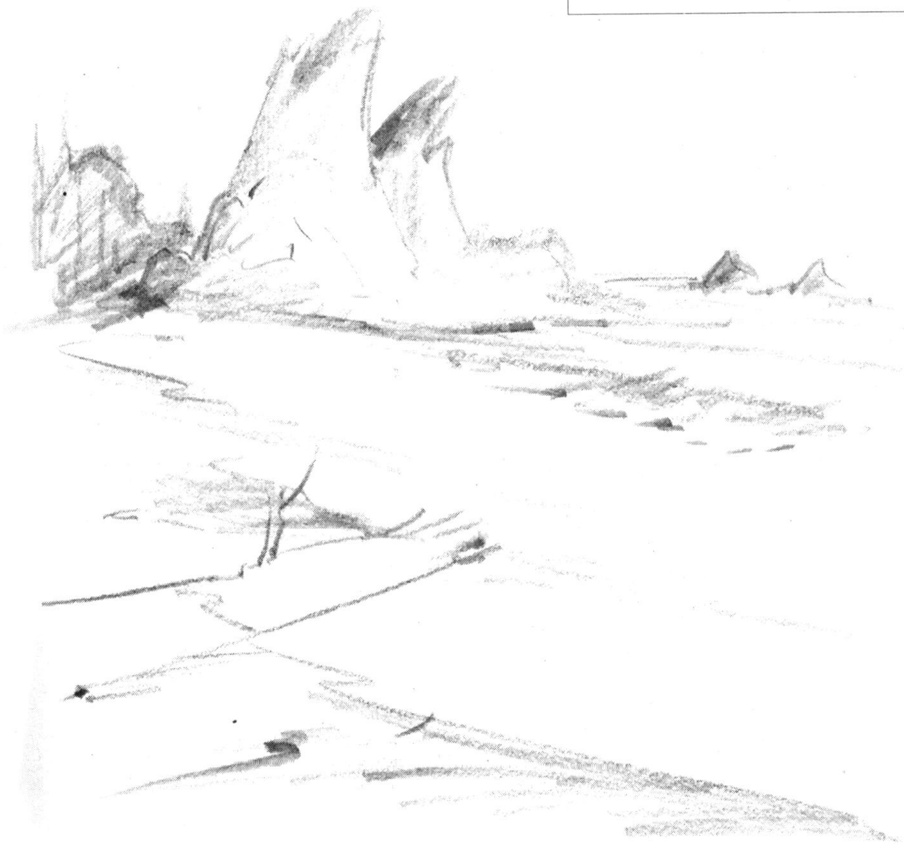

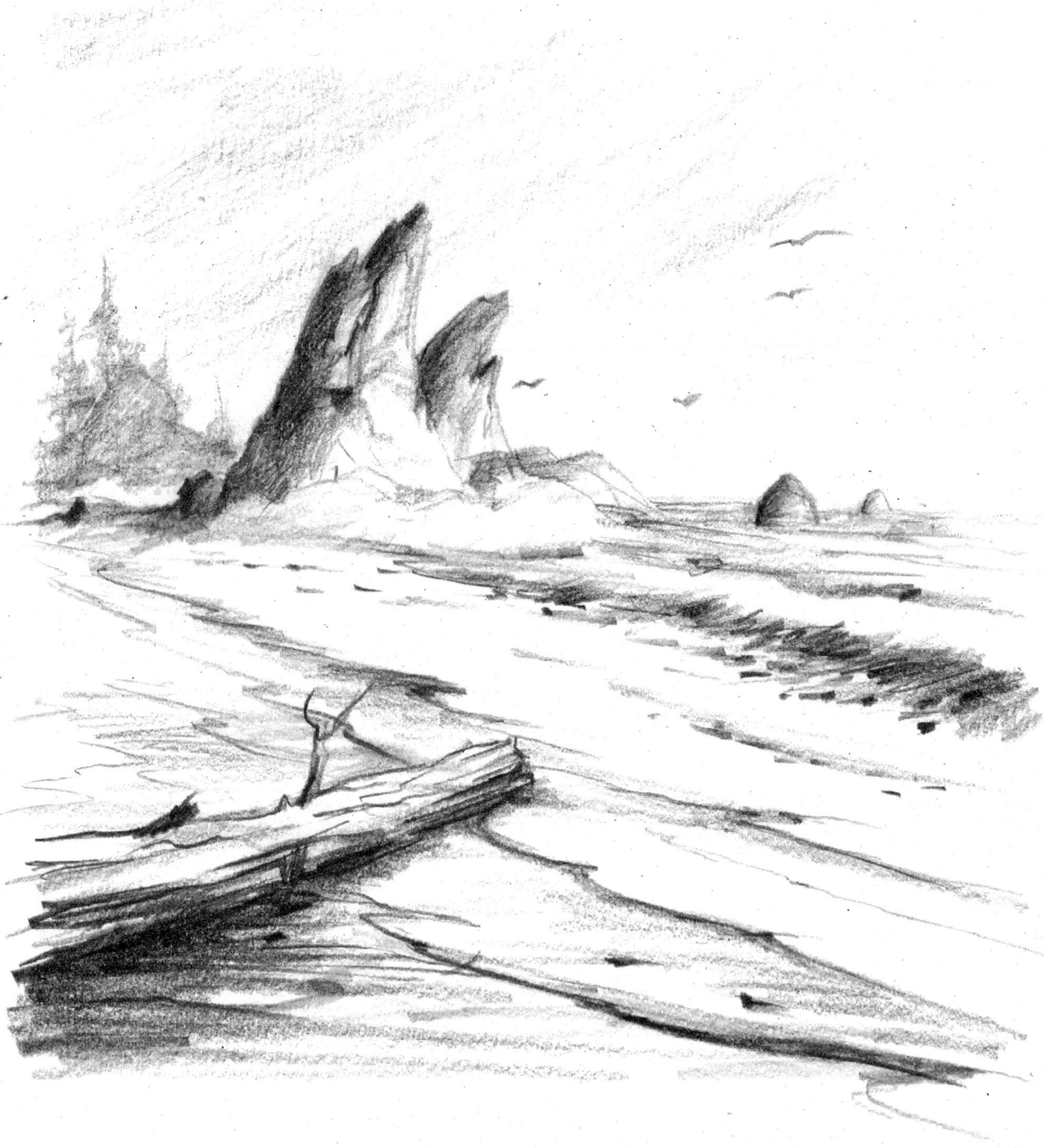

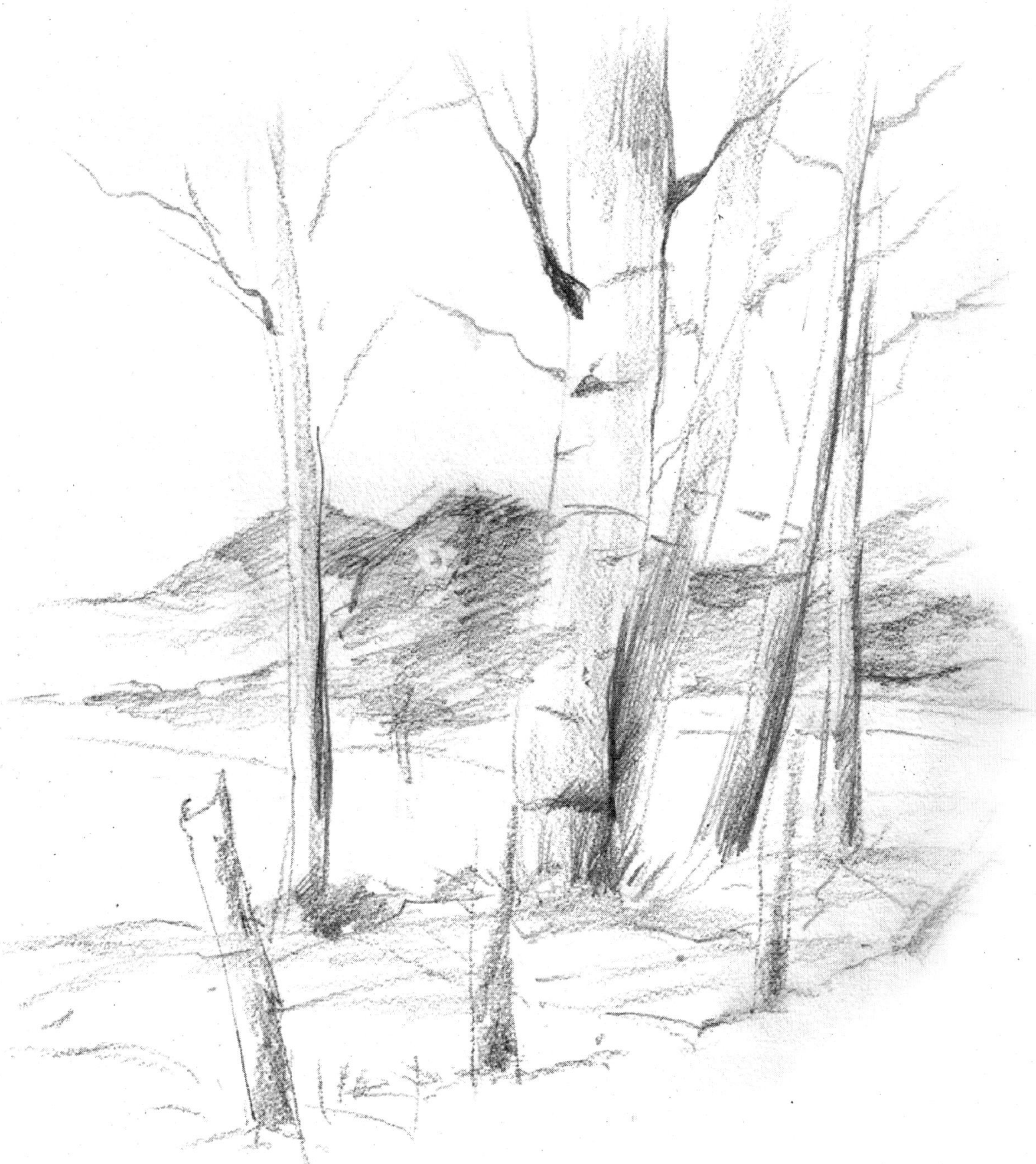

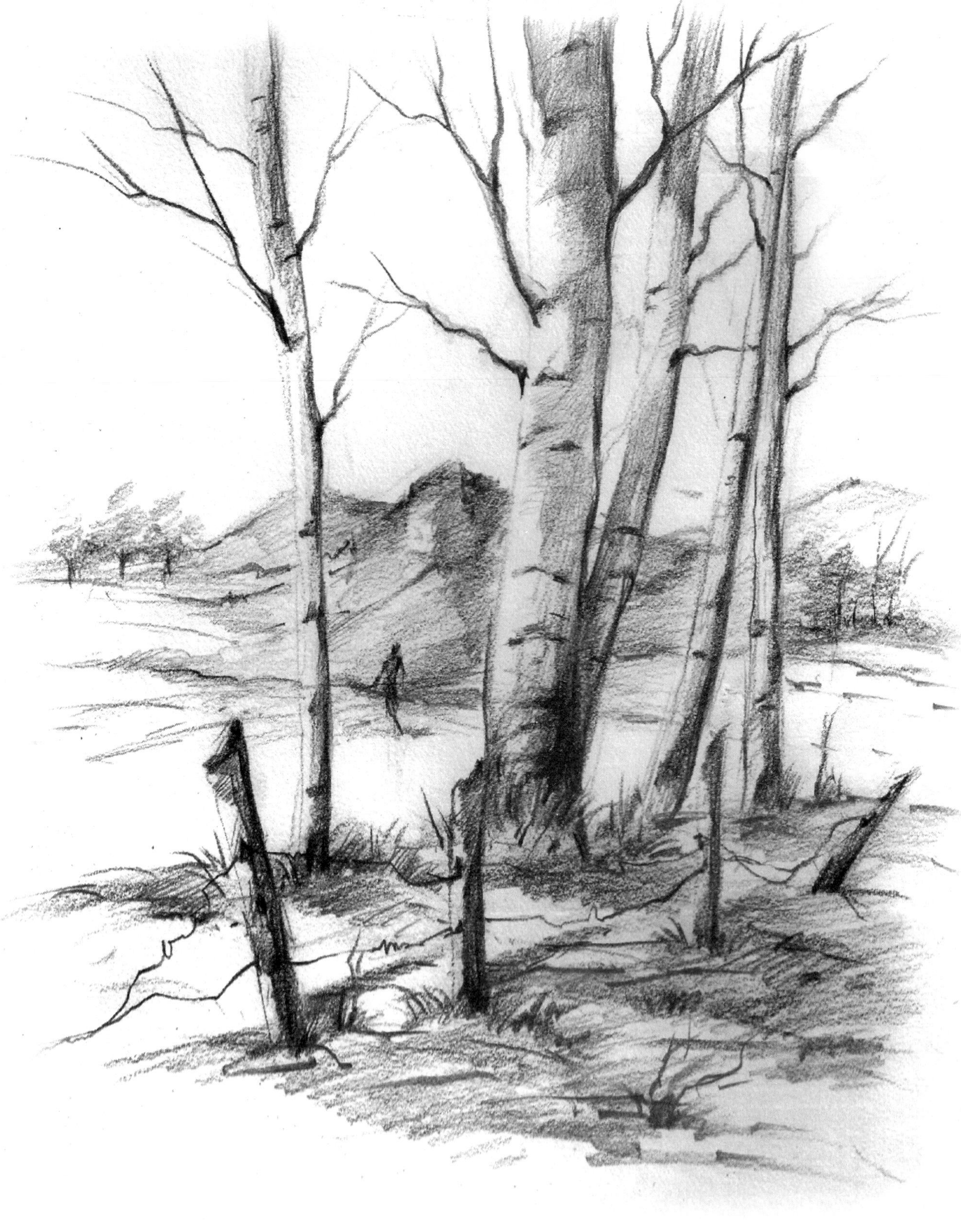

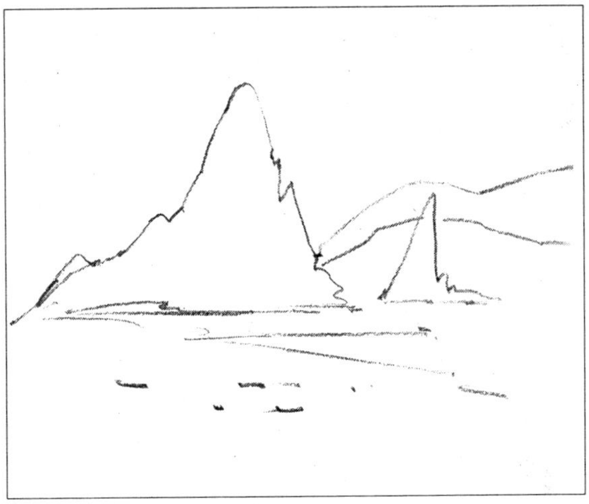

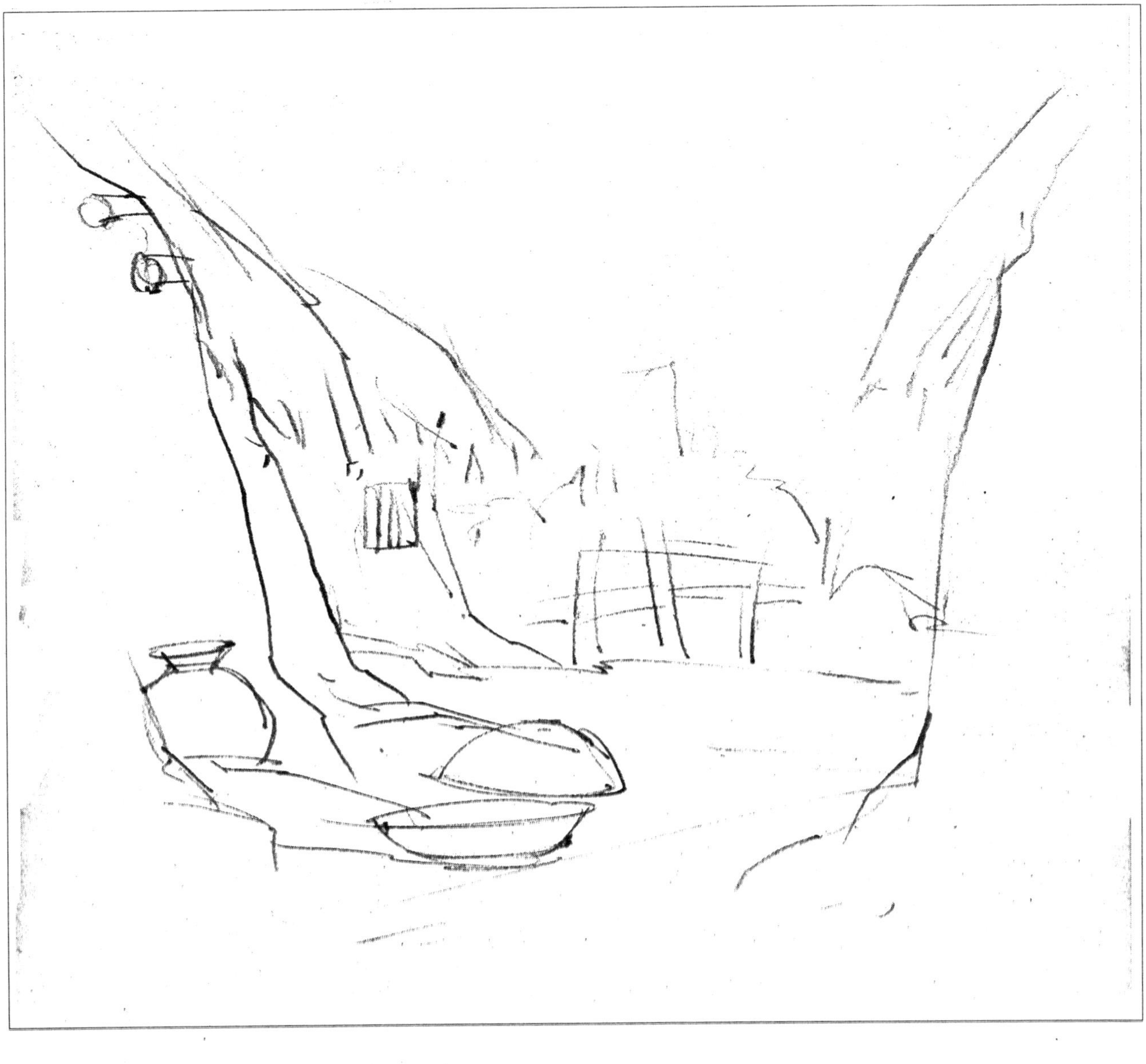

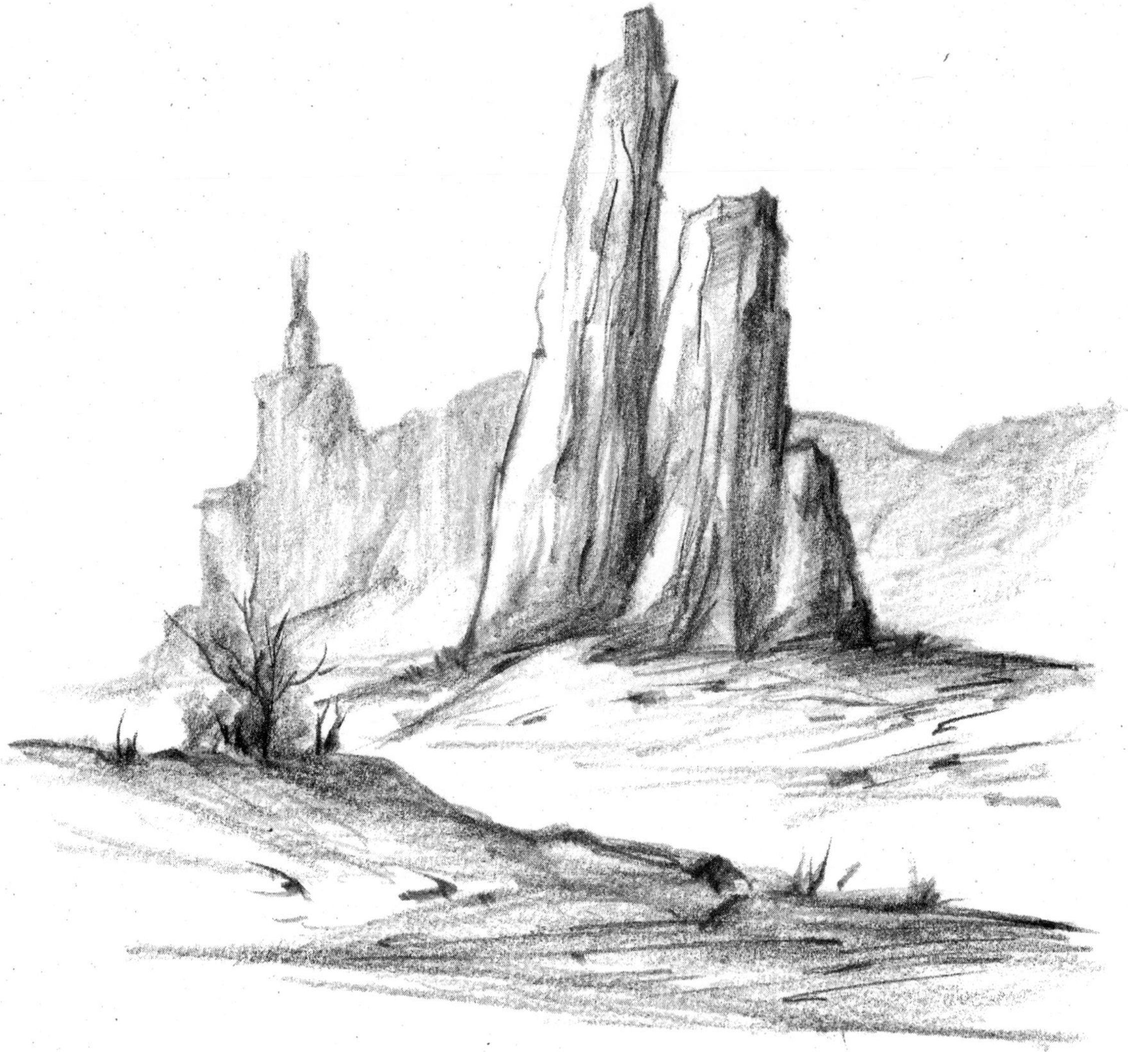

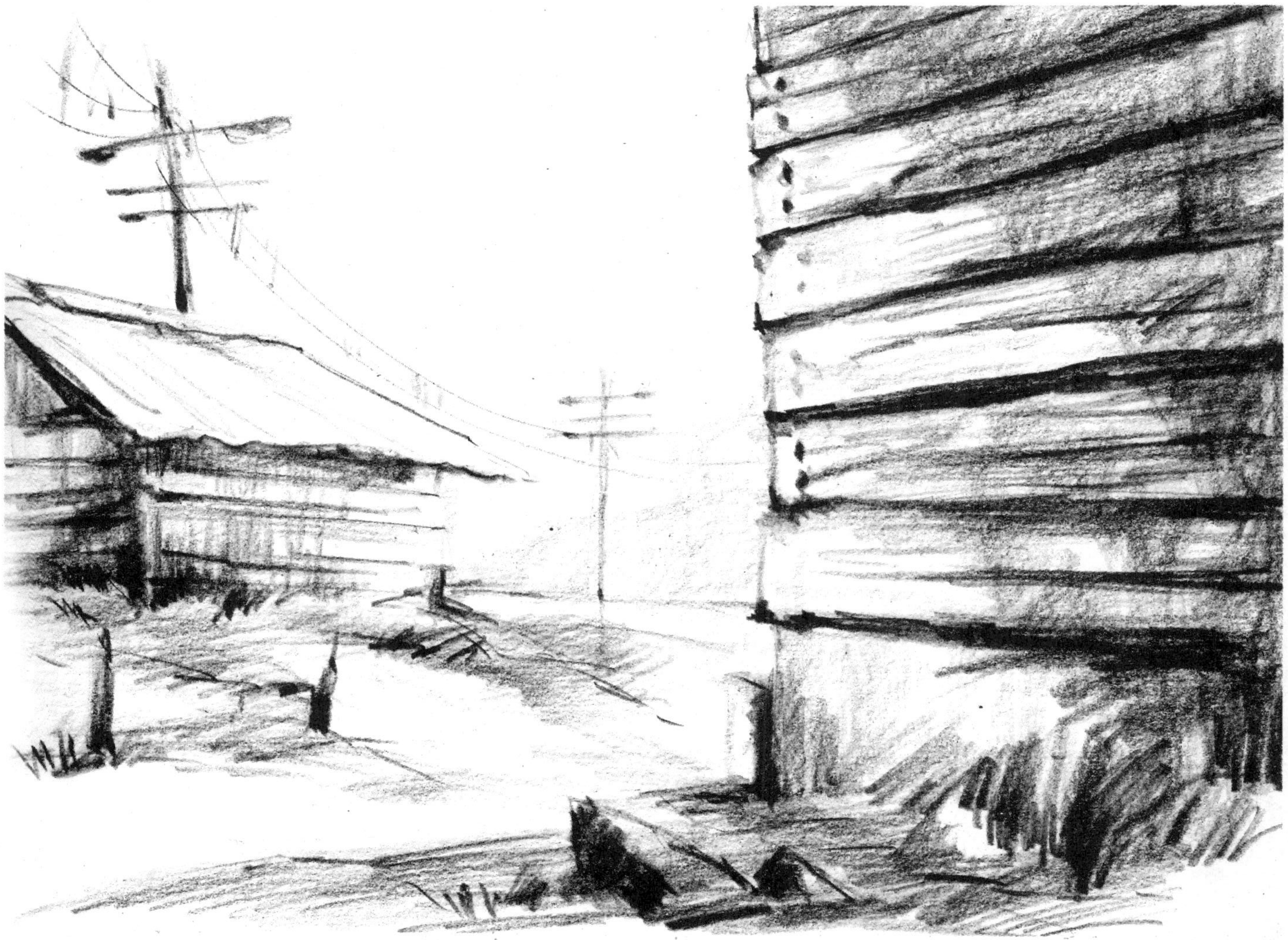

In this picture the main subject is a wood house. Here the wood texture and the tonal variation has been shown. Here the source of light is created from the right hand side of the picture and the shadow is shown opposite to the source of light.

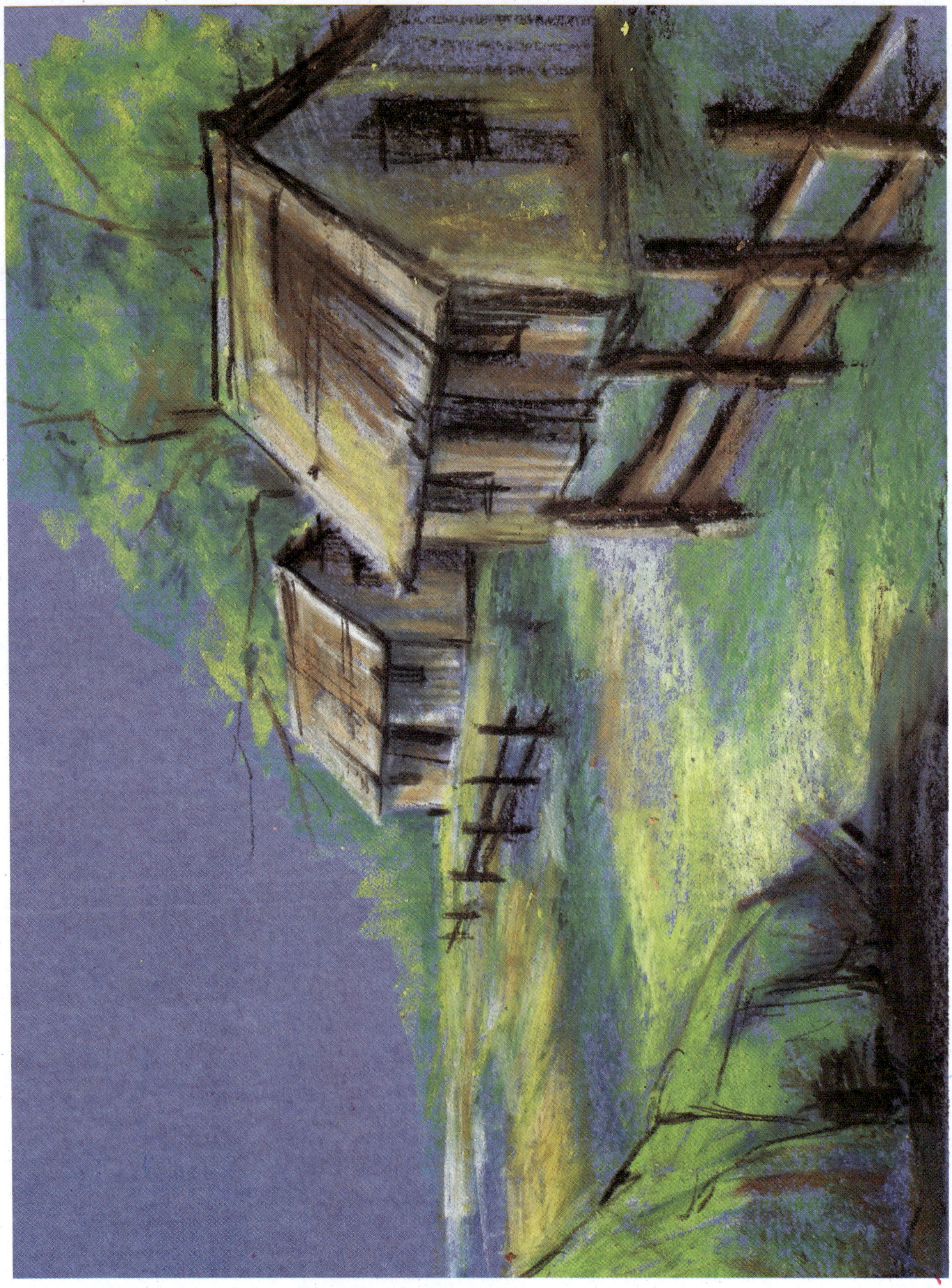

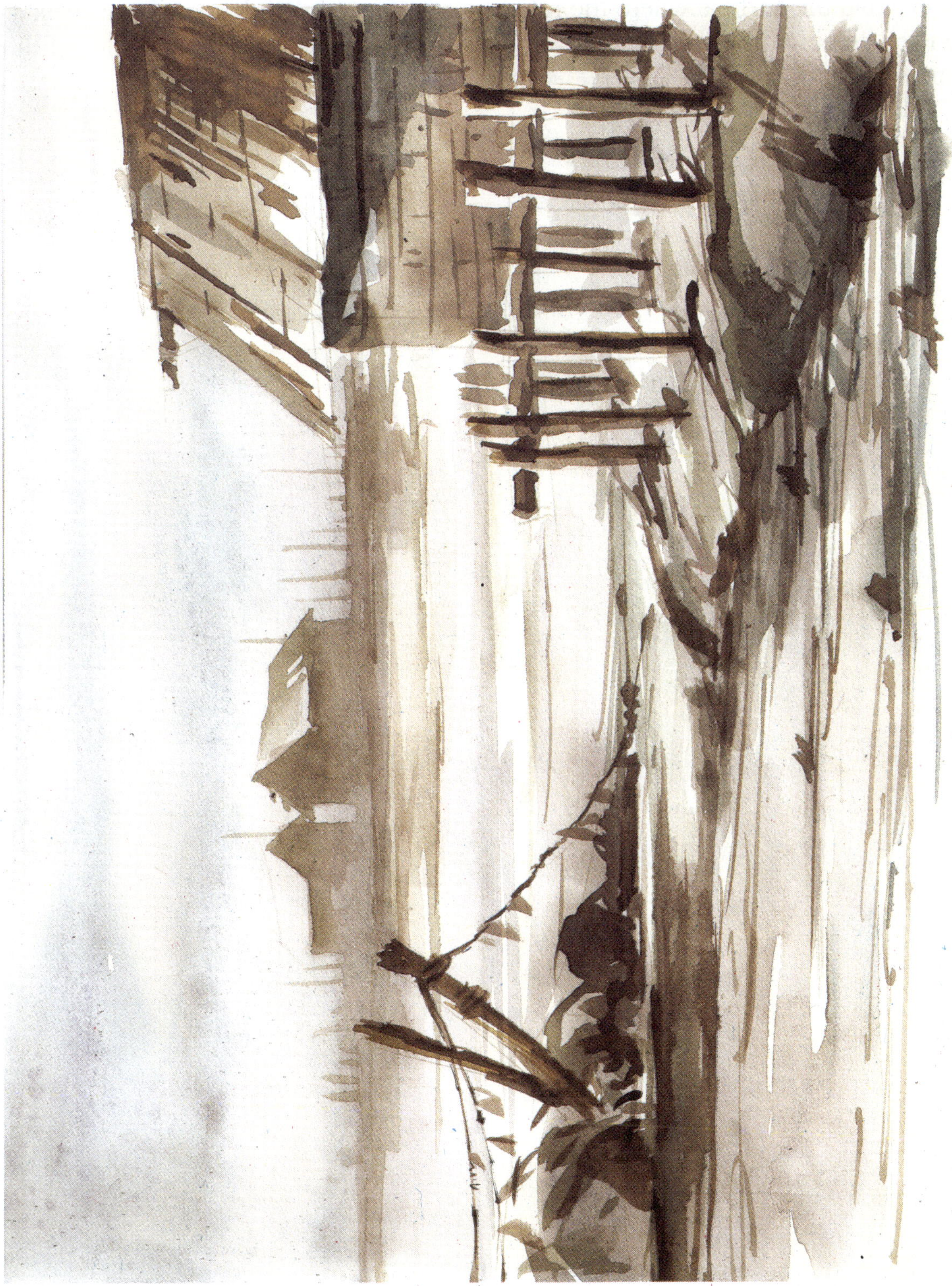

Shadow

In many cases we tend to use shadow in landscape drawing. In this case then, we should understand the surface where the reflection is created. While using, the strokes should be used technically. We should also observe the material as the character of the shadow depends on it.

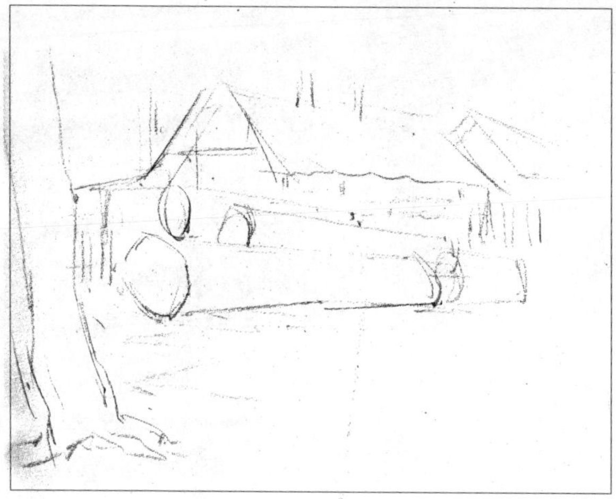

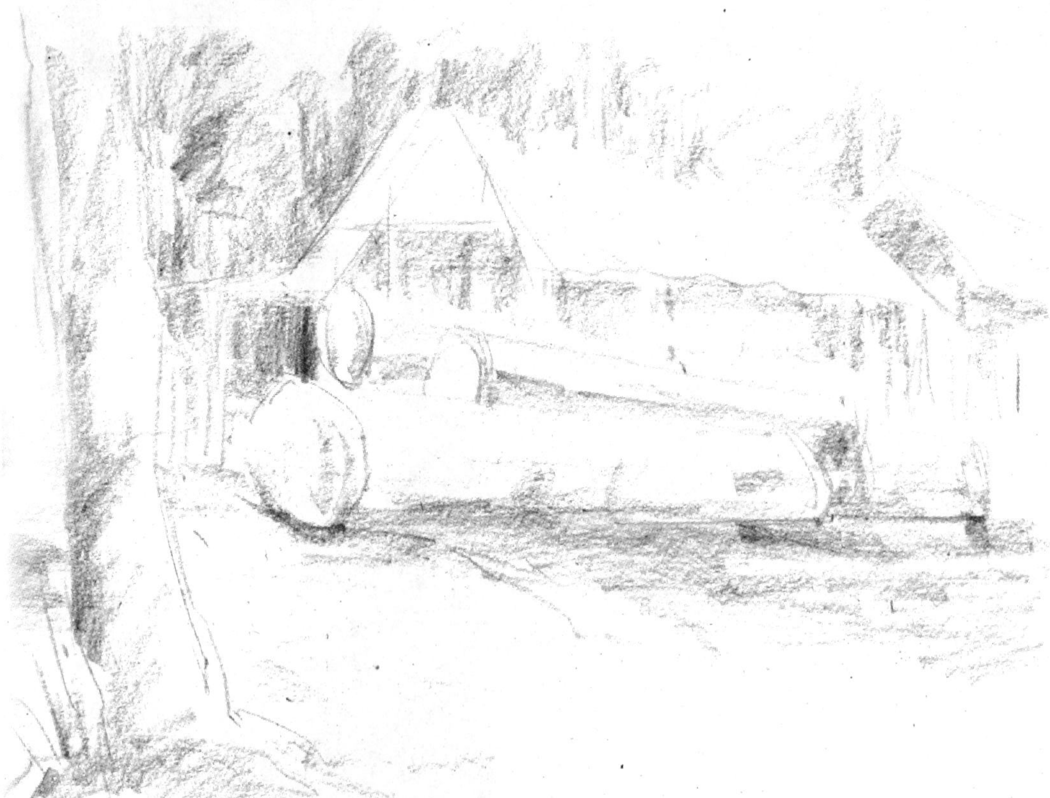

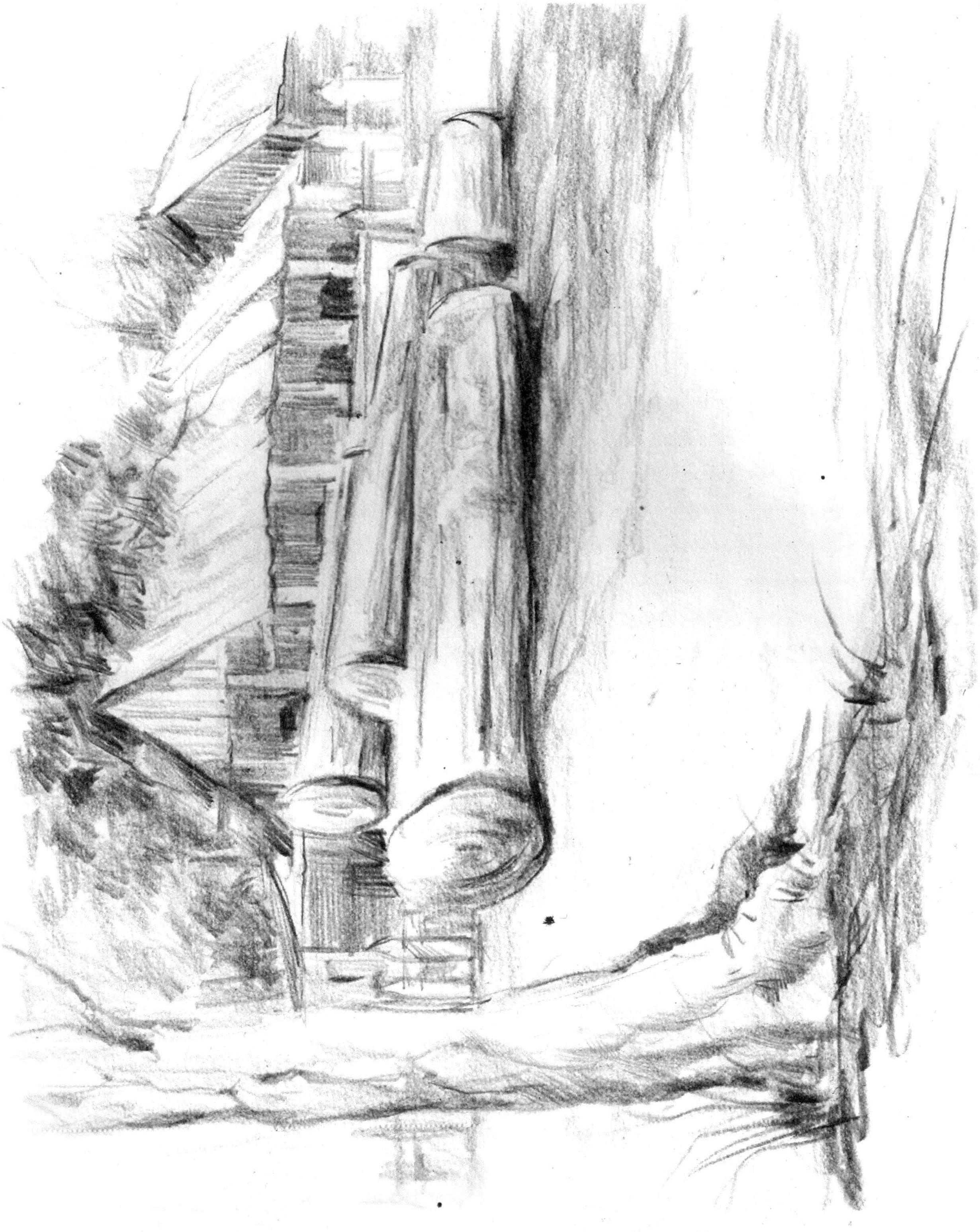

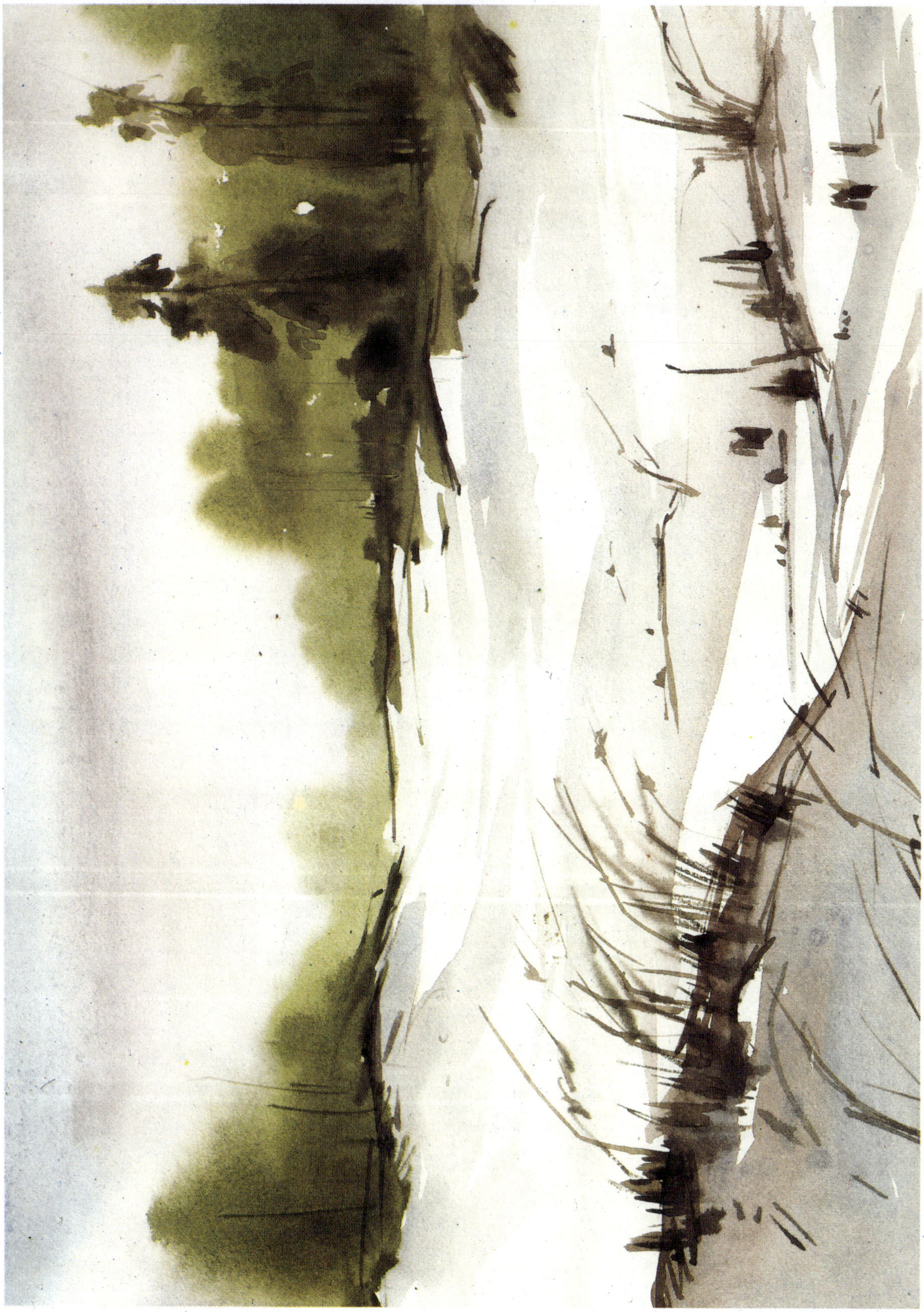

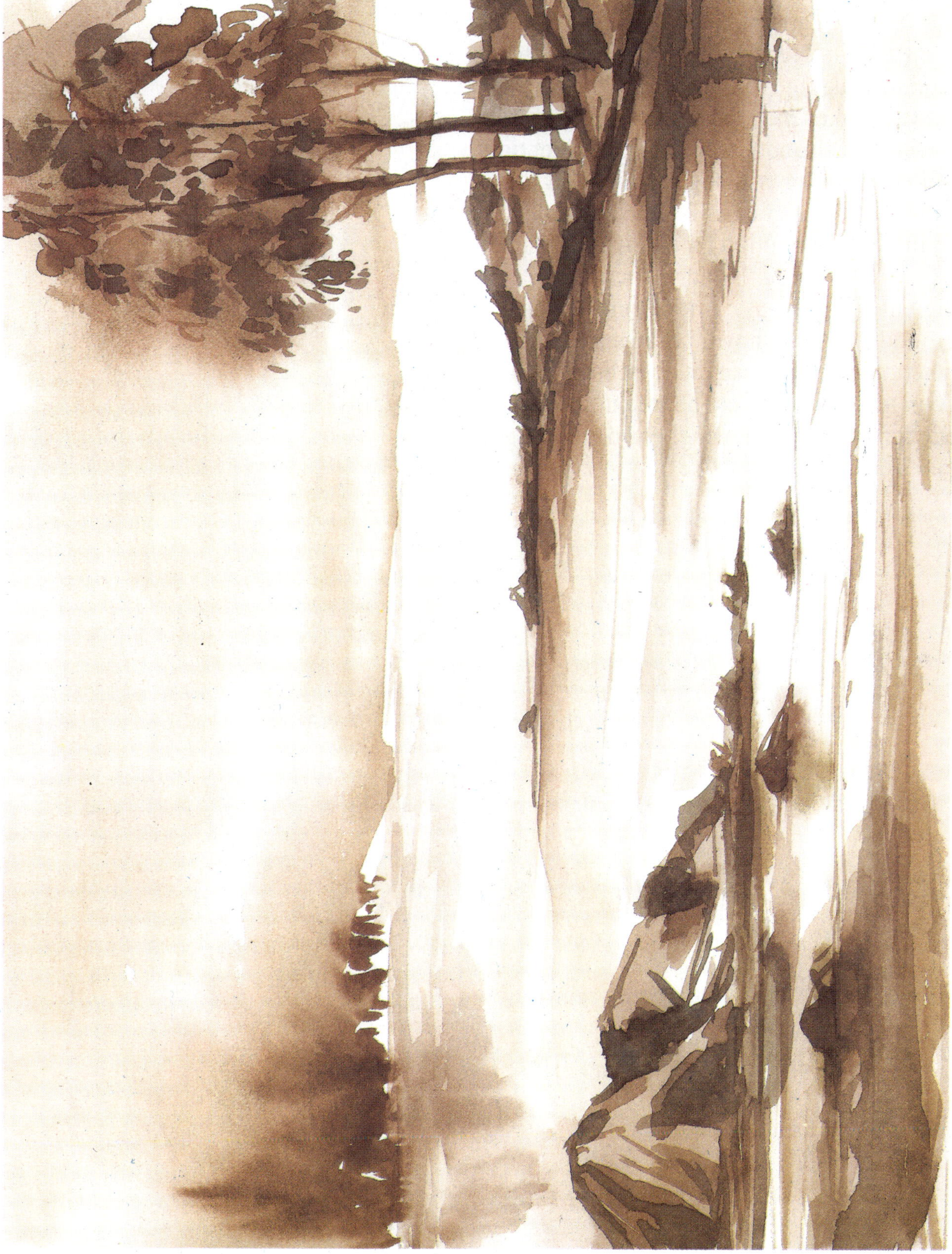

In this landscape picture, a village scene has been shown. Here the subjects are the huts And to make the mud walls visible, the pencil strokes have been used softly. Taking the help of the source of light the direction of pencil stroke is changed. As the light source of the picture is from right hand side, so the light reflection on the huts on the left hand side is more. Besides, the backside of the hut is shown using dark tone. In the ground we have shown baskets and a pot where the pencil stroke's character has been depicted particularly. The tree in the far background has been suggested using light tones of the pencil strokes.

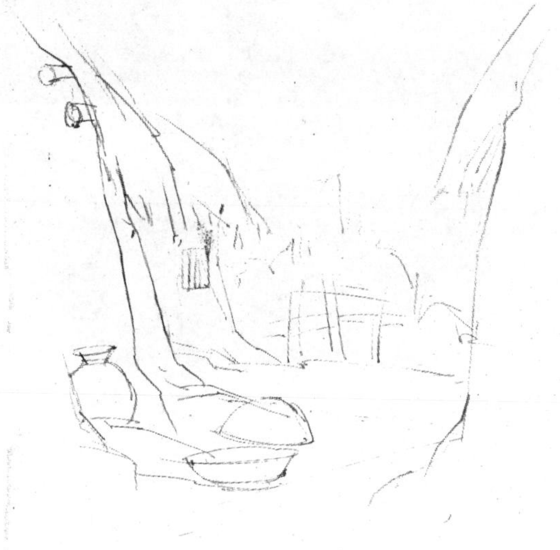

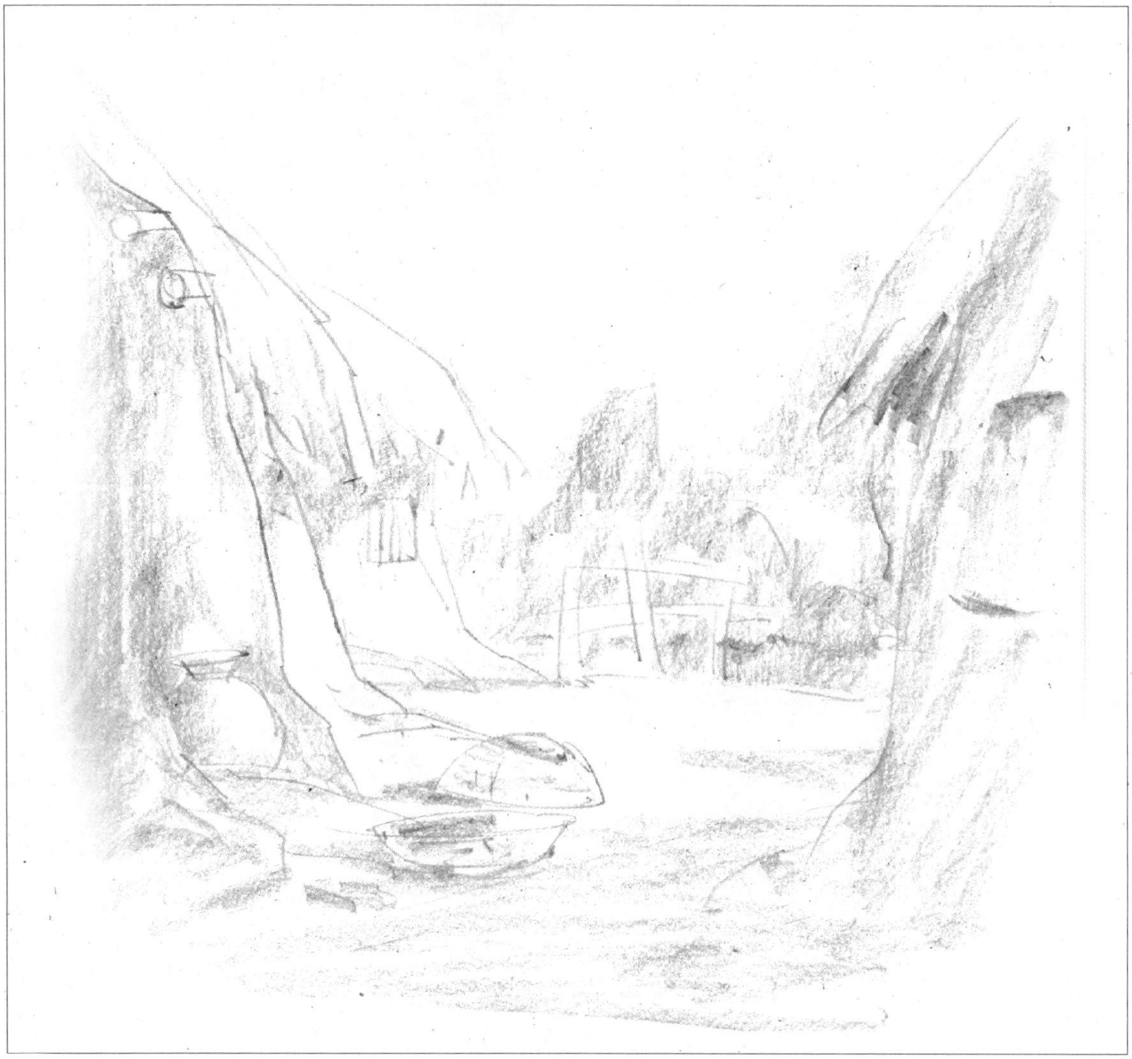

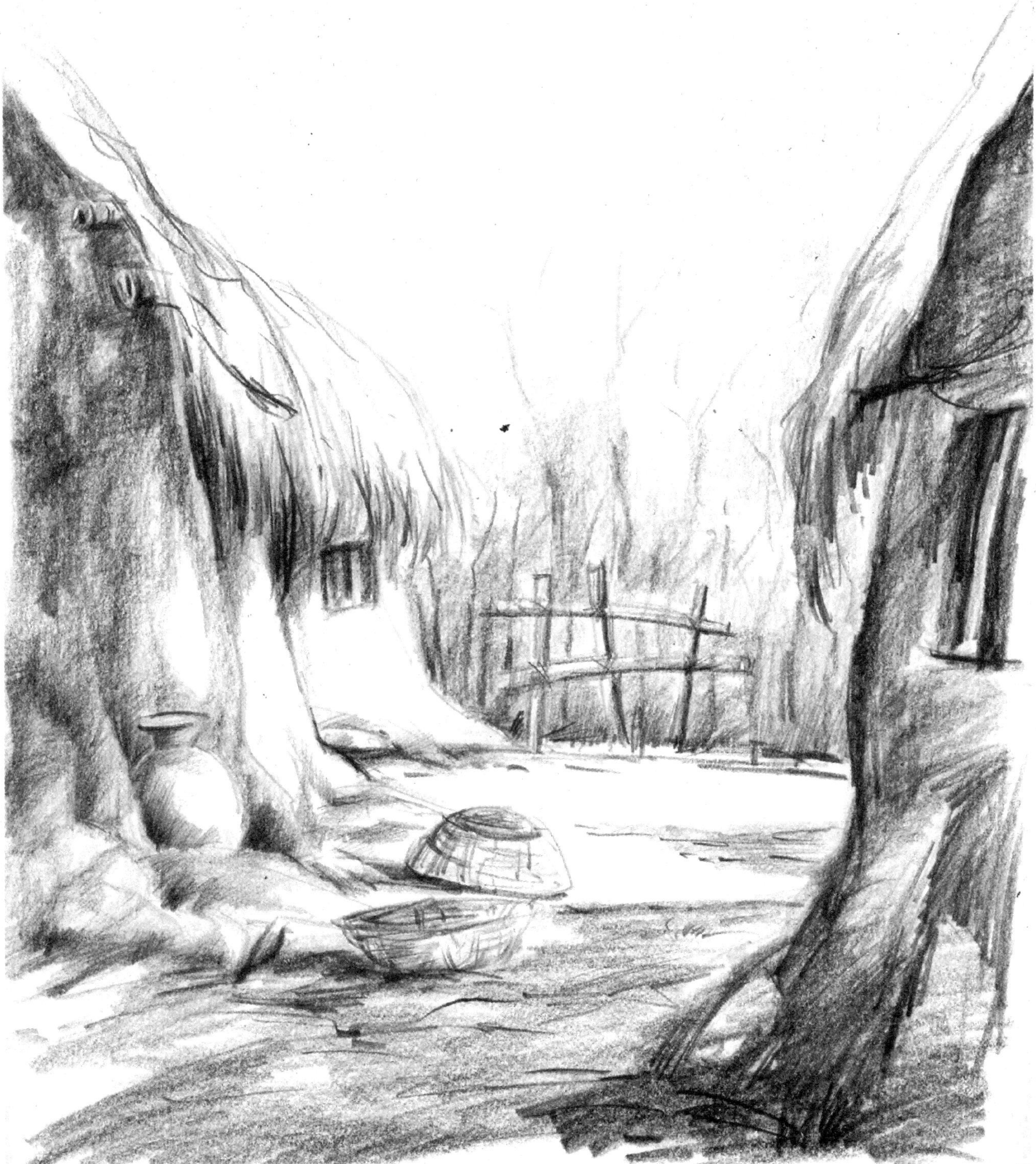

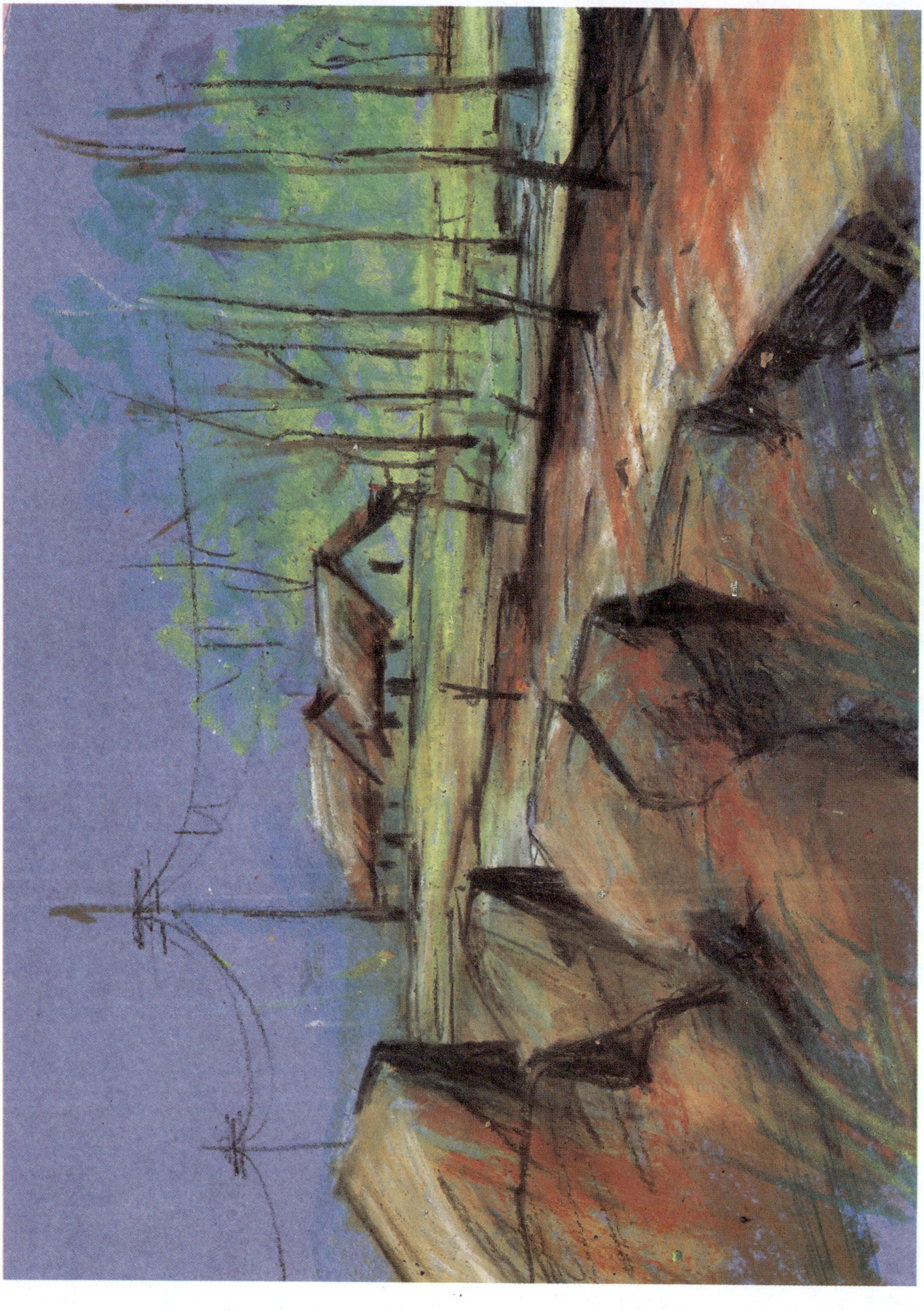

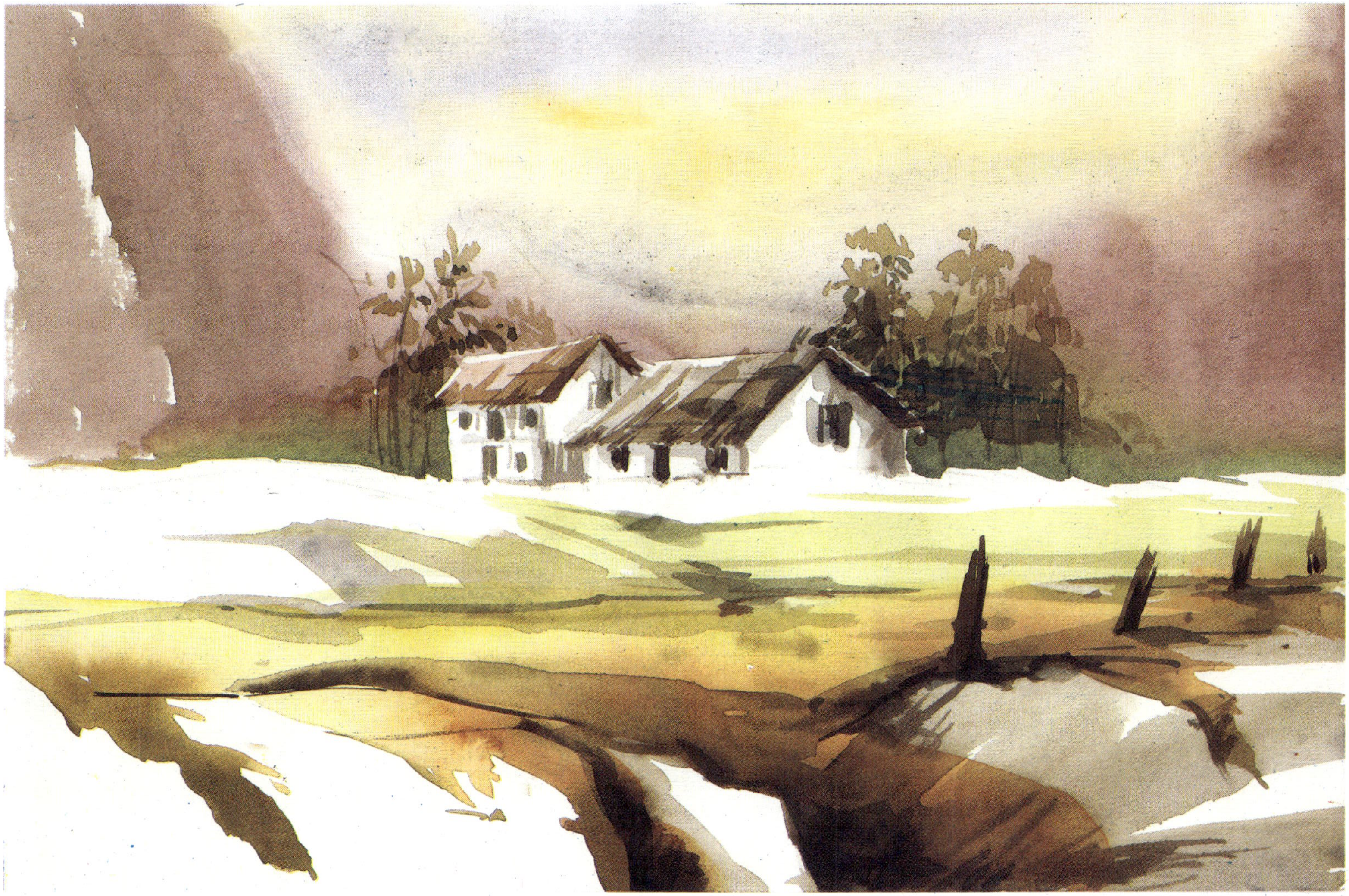

You've seen this picture earlier. You must have done a painting similar to this one. Here the paper has been damped first, after which the sky has been painted. Prussian blue and sap green has been used to depict the green background. In the foreground the hut and greenery has been shown using paper white and tonal variation. Colours used are burnt sienna, ultra marine blue, yellow ochre and vermilion red.

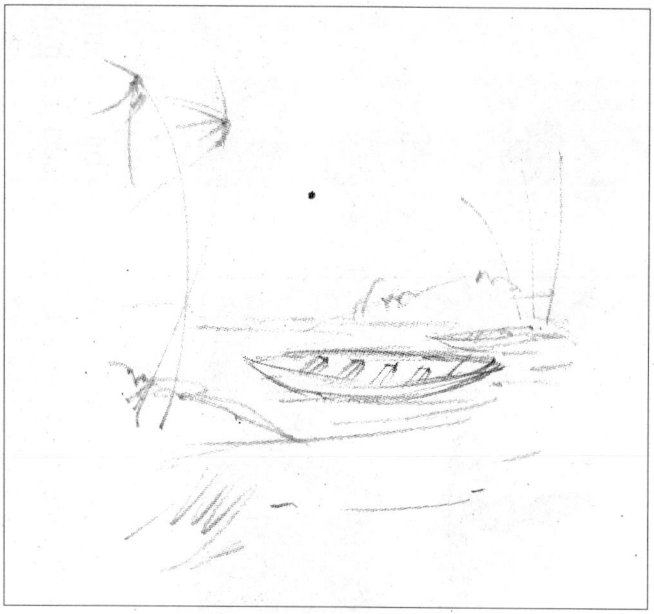

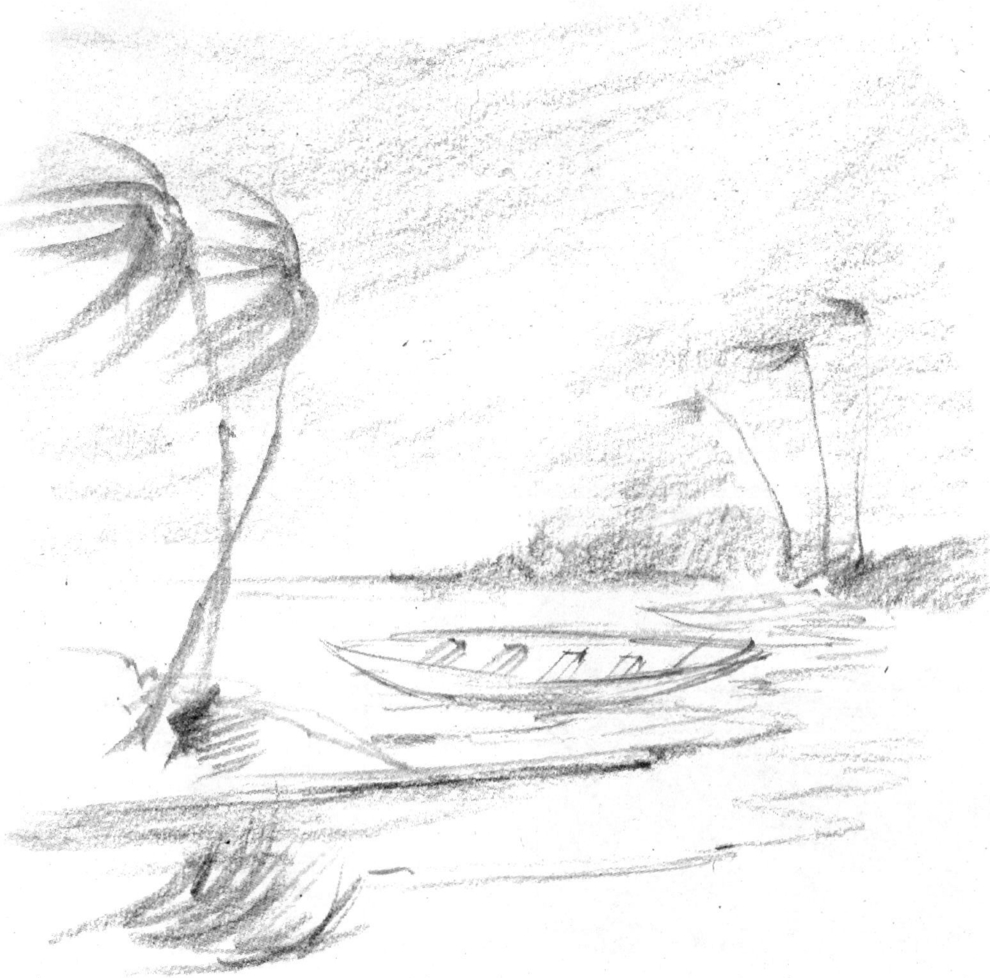

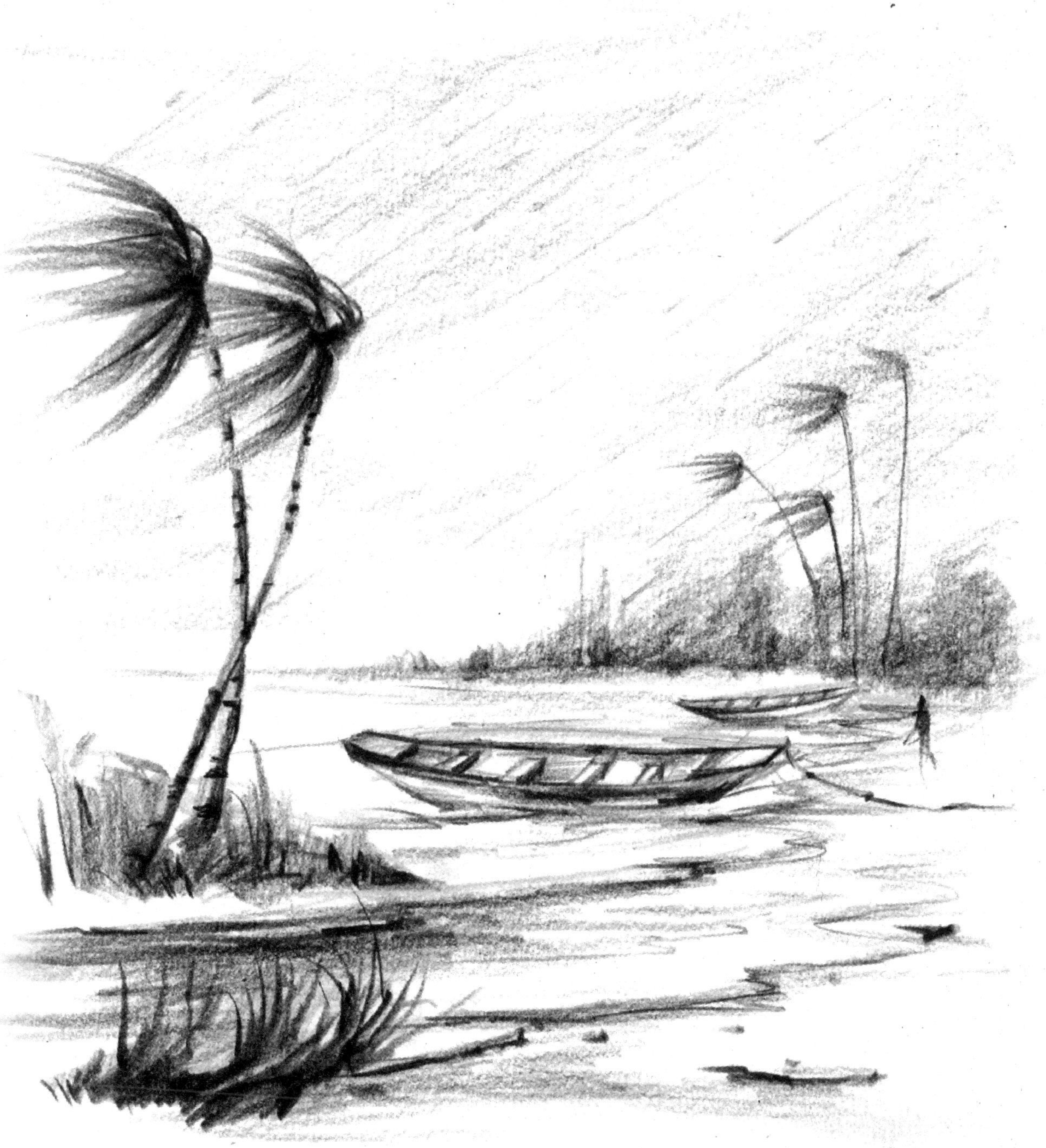

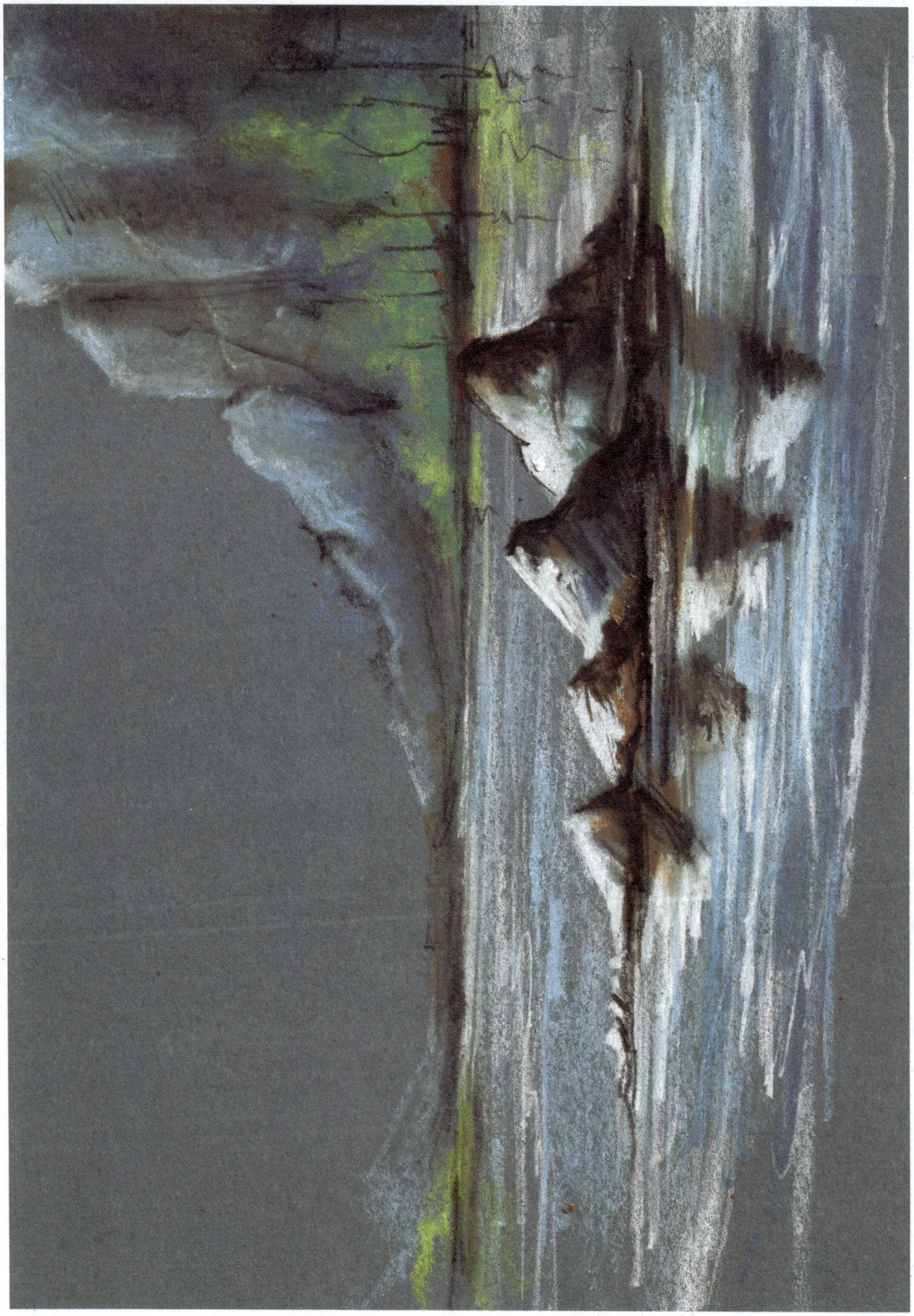

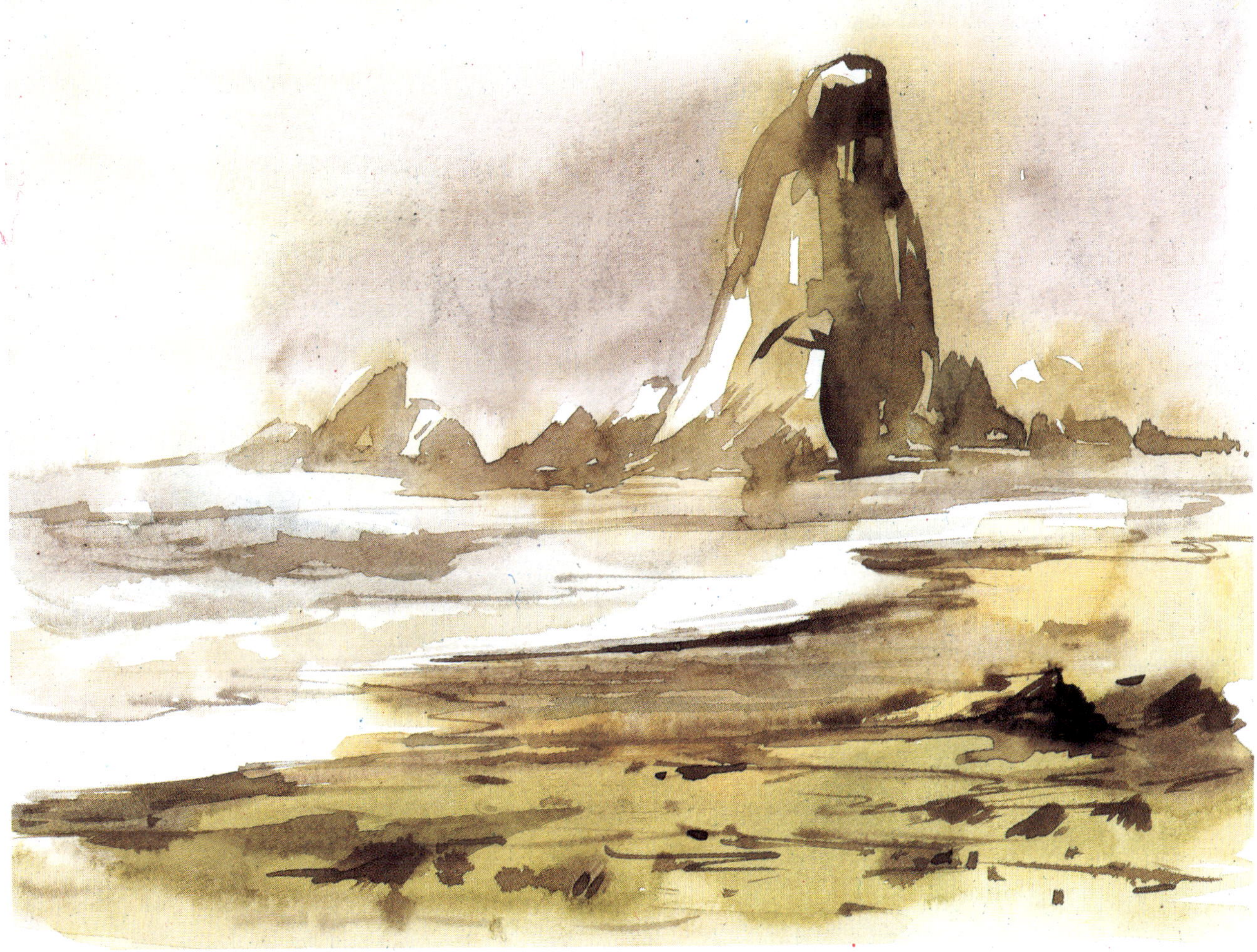

1) Start with a yellow ochre under painting and let dry. 2) Paint in the sky and drop in green colour into the wet wash near the horizon. Later, the mountain will be painted in around the soft edges to form the distance foliage. 3) Add washes on either side to establish the water. Light areas are lifted from the mountains with a moist one-inch brush. 4) Paint in closest range of mountains and add detail on either side of the road. Add shadows to enhance the feeling of light.

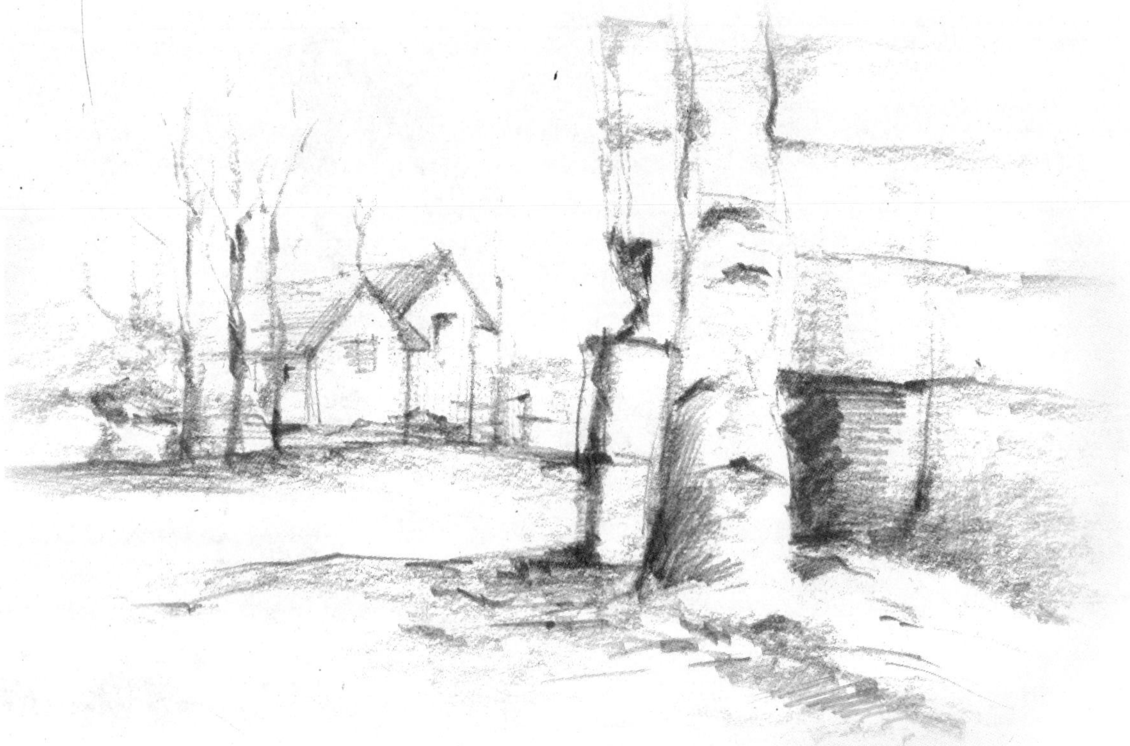

Practice makes a man perfect, so does hard work. So, best of luck while you keep embarking on new journeys and reach and achieve different goals and targets. So good luck to you all and keep drawing and practicing new techniques.